MAKING DOLLS
FOR PLEASURE & PROFIT

ANITA HOLMES
MAKING DOLLS
FOR PLEASURE & PROFIT

ARCO PUBLISHING COMPANY, INC.

NEW YORK

Published 1978 by Arco Publishing Company, Inc.
219 Park Avenue South, New York, N.Y. 10003

Library of Congress Cataloging in Publication Data
Holmes, Anita
    Making dolls for pleasure & profit

    1. Dollmaking.   I. Title.
TT175.H 65   1978   745.59'22   77-25288
ISBN 0-668-04534-5

Acknowledgment
I would like to thank Pollock's Toy Museum for the loan of the
old toys used in the illustrations and all friends who have
encouraged and helped me over the last few months.

Photographs by James Holmes

Designed by Melvyn Gill Design Associates

Printed in Great Britain

CONTENTS

INTRODUCTION

Although I have been making soft toys and rag dolls for several years, I only became interested in the craft of dollmaking when I discovered a German doll, made in 1880. This old doll had a kid body with a bisque head and composition arms and legs. I wanted to make a modern version of it, but all in cloth so that children could play with it without spoiling it in any way.

After working out a body pattern that resembled the original, I designed the head, arms and legs to suit it. The limbs were particularly challenging because the methods used for constructing the joints in the German doll could not be applied to an all-cloth doll, as I learned by trial and error!

When I came to the making-up stage my experience with rag dolls was of little help. To start with, it was impossible to stitch the pieces by machine without losing the detailed shape and the strength that I wanted, and so I had to hand sew. Another problem was finding materials which would be tough, washable and, at the same time, attractive. Initially, I bought bleached calico and dyed it, but the results looked artificial. Unbleached calico proved to be the answer, with kapok as a stuffing. This gave me the correct degree of firmness, and the faint show-through of the kapok produced just the flesh tone I was seeking.

After many months of perfecting my first design I had become so fascinated by this craft that I went on to study the styles of doll and methods of construction used by dollmakers of different periods and countries. From this research grew the collection presented here.

Whether you are an experienced needlewoman or a beginner, you will be able to reproduce any of the dolls in this book. Each pattern is printed actual size so that it can be traced, thus ensuring absolute accuracy of cut and dispensing with the complicated procedure of transferring the design to graph paper. The instructions include numerous small details which give the dolls their unique personalities, making them such fun to make.

When you have made a doll remember, please, that it was designed for children to play with. So do let them!

1. MAKING THE DOLLS

Equipment and Materials

The equipment and materials used for dollmaking are simple and inexpensive. All the stitching is by hand, therefore you do not even require a sewing machine.

Before you start on your first doll collect together all the items listed below.

1 Sharp HB lead pencil.
2 Tracing or greaseproof paper.
3 Firm paper for making the patterns. Wrapping or writing paper would be suitable if it is sufficiently thick to withstand being used several times.
4 Scissors. You will need scissors for cutting paper as well as sharp dressmaking shears.
5 Unbleached calico. The quantity required is given with the instructions for making each doll and is for 92cm wide fabric. I recommend this material because it is strong, keeps its shape well when stuffed and is inexpensive. Also, it does not require dying since it is a quite realistic flesh colour. When buying calico ask for the standard grade or, if there is a choice, the calico with the closest weave.
6 Sewing thread. Choose a very pale pink thread, since all your stitches will be visible. Coats' Drima or Gütermann Spun Polyester are both recommended because they have plenty of 'give' in them and are therefore unlikely to snap during stuffing.
7 Tape measure.
8 Thimble.
9 Needles. You need fine needles for all the sewing apart from the hair for which you must have medium and large darning needles.
10 Stuffing. I suggest that you use 'Pure Airspanded Kapok'. In my experience it is the best material on the market for this purpose as it always gives good results. I was warned not to wash kapok but, after successful experimentation, I discussed the problem with the manufacturers and found

that kapok stands up to washing without adverse effects. It is sold in minimum quantities of 200g (½lb) and so I have stipulated 200g for some of the dolls, even though you may not use the whole amount. A 400g bag is, of course, cheaper. Should you have any difficulty in obtaining kapok, contact the U.S. distributor who will supply minimum orders to you direct. Their address is: Royal Manufacturing Corporation, Box 5155, Charlotte, North Carolina 28225.

11 Dressmaker's pins.

12 Small wooden spoon or a similar implement with a rounded handle for pressing down the kapok. You can use the blunt end of a knitting needle, but be careful that the knob does not catch on the kapok and pull it out again.

13 Yarn for the hair. Any type of wool, cotton or silk yarn can be used [see p. 17].

14 Embroidery silks. These are used for the eyelids, lashes, brows and nostrils [see p. 15].

15 Nail varnish. A pink shade for the lips and finger nails and blue, green or brown shade for the eyes.

16 Indian ink. This is for the pupils of the eyes, although you can use black thread if you prefer.

17 Face powder, either loose or compacted. I have found that blushing the dolls' cheeks with powder makes the faces far more realistic.

18 A dowel 12mm [½in] in diameter, 43.5cm [17in] long. This is primarily for the stick doll, but it is also useful for making curls [see p. 18].

19 Elastic 5mm [$\frac{3}{16}$in] wide. Used for the jointed doll.

20 Four strong, shanked buttons, line 24 [⅝in]. Used for the jointed doll.

21 Fine steel crochet hook. This, too, is required primarily for the jointed doll, but it is also useful for stuffing all the dolls' thumbs.

The stitches

To achieve the best results with your dolls keep all stitching — whether visible or not — as small, neat and even as you can.

For those of you who may be unfamiliar with hand sewing, all the stitches used in this book are given below.

Backstitch

A strong stitch used to join two pieces together on the wrong side of the work. Each top stitch should be the same length and each bottom stitch twice the length of the top stitches. The finished line resembles straight machine sewing.

Side and rear of Peg Doll shows simple construction of joints.

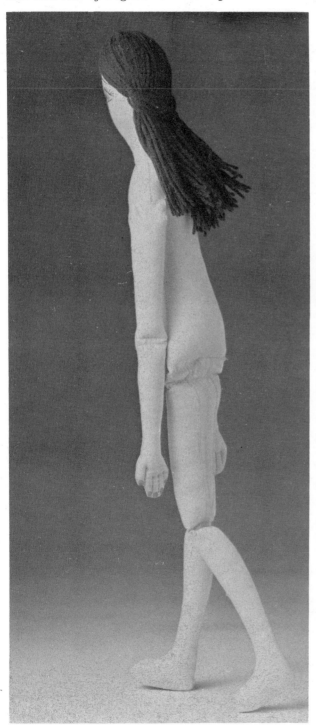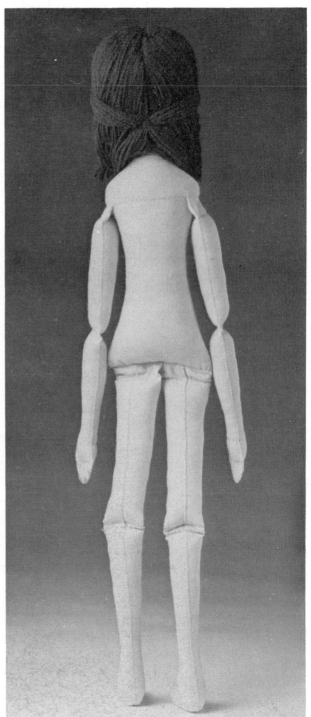

Fig 37

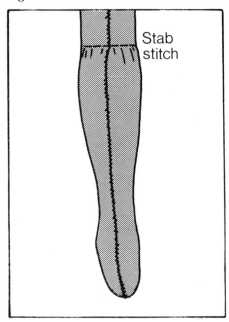

Stab
stitch

2 Pull the body and arms down over the head and, on the right side, whip the seam.
3 Stuff the head and shoulders very tightly. Be careful to keep the neck straight and firm so that it cannot wobble.
4 Push the kapok right up into each shoulder and stuff the body as tightly as you can.
5 Turn in the raw edge at the bottom of the body and oversew the front and back together from side seam to side seam.

The legs

1 Stuff the feet and legs up to the knees.
2 Taking one leg at a time, hold the front and back seams together at the centre of the knee. Make a line of stabbing stitch across one half of the leg and then across the other [see figure 37].
3 Sew another line parallel to and 7mm [¼in] from the first.
4 Continue stuffing to within 2.5cm [1in] of the opening, then make another line of stabbing stitch as for the knee.
5 Turn in the raw edges 5mm [⅜in] and oversew.
6 Work the other leg in the same way.
7 Stitch the top seams of the legs to the bottom seam of the body [see figure 38] by oversewing first along the fronts and then the backs.

Bringing your doll to life

Following the instructions given in Chapter Two, work the face and hair.

Add the finishing touch by painting the tips of the fingers and thumbs with pink nail varnish.

Dressing your doll

From the basic garment patterns you can make a variety of clothes for your doll. When made up in blue, the outfit turns from a guard's to a policeman's uniform or, in a printed fabric, into a girl's trouser suit. By lengthening the patterns you can make a coat from the jacket and a nightdress from the blouse. The pinafore dress can be cut to any length you like from a mini to a maxi. To make a beach outfit, take the bodice of the pinafore for a sun top and shorten the trouser pattern to make a pair of shorts.

Fig 38

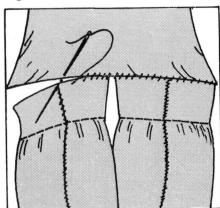

GIRL'S OUTFIT

As illustrated on p. 27.

Materials required

Petticoat and pants
40cm of white lawn
Four small white buttons
1.20m of narrow white lace

Pinafore dress
50cm of printed cotton
Two matching buttons
75cm of ribbon

Blouse
25cm plain poplin
Four small matching buttons
25cm of 5mm elastic

Boots
Small pieces of leather
1m of narrow ribbon

Cutting out the pattern
Following the preparation instructions given on p. 22, cut out
the pattern pieces.

Sewing
Sew 5mm [$\frac{3}{16}$in] in from the raw edges

Petticoat

The bodice
1 Backstitch all the shoulder seams to make two separate
   bodices [one bodice to form the lining]. Press open all the
   seams.
2 With their right sides together join the bodices along the neck
   and back opening with a small running stitch. Turn to right
   side and press.
3 Backstitch the side seams of each bodice separately.
4 For the armhole binding, cut a strip of material on the bias
   [on the cross] 13mm [½in] in width. Press in the side edges
   and bind the two armholes [see figure 39].

The skirt
1 Cut one length of material 25.5cm × 45.5cm [10in × 18in],
   and another piece 6.5cm × 76cm [2½in × 30in] for the
   frill.
2 Using a long running stitch gather one edge of the frill

Fig 39

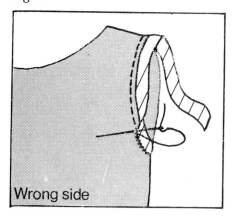

Wrong side

length to fit the skirt. Backstitch the edges together.

3 With the backstitched seam facing you, fold down the skirt material to cover it and hem the bottom fold line to your original stitching line [see figure 40].

4 Join the centre back of the skirt and the frill with a french seam [see p. 21], leaving 12.5cm [5in] open at the top. Fold in and hem the edges of this opening.

5 Gather the waist of the skirt to fit the bodice. Backstitch the bodice and skirt together leaving the bodice lining loose [see p. 22].

6 Turn up the bodice lining and hem it down to enclose this seam.

7 Work three evenly-spaced buttonloops [see p. 22] on one edge of the back bodice and sew the buttons into position.

8 On the right side of the skirt, just above the frill join, make three tucks with a small running stitch [see figure 41]. Press them towards the hem.

9 Turn up and hem the frill.

10 Sew the lace, edge to edge, along the bottom of the hem and round the frill seam.

Pants

1 French seam the centre back join, turn in and hem down the two centre front edges.

2 Make a french seam round the inside legs. Turn up and hem the bottoms.

3 For the waistband, cut a strip of material on the bias 2cm × 12.5cm [¾in × 5in].

4 With a running stitch gather the top of the pants to fit the doll and, with the right sides together, backstitch the waistband to the pants along the gather line.

5 Fold the waistband to the inside over the seam, turn in the raw edges and hem them down.

6 Make a buttonloop at one end of the waistband and sew a button onto the other end.

7 Stitch the lace, edge to edge, along the bottom of the leg hems.

Blouse

1 Backstitch all the shoulder and side seams to make two separate blouses [one blouse to form the lining]. Press open all the seams.

2 With the right sides together, join the two bodices with a small running stitch along the neck and back opening edges. Turn right side out and press.

3 Join the sleeves with french seams. Press the seams to one side.

Fig 40

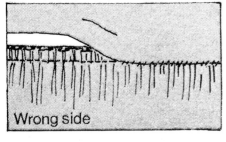

Fig 41

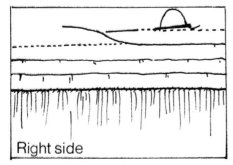

4 Gather the tops of the sleeves to fit the bodice armholes and backstitch them to the bodice, leaving the bodice lining loose [see p. 21]. Turn inside out and hem the armholes of the lining down to enclose the seams.

5 Turn up the bottom edges of the blouse and, on the right side, neatly oversew them together.

6 Make a 7mm [½in] hem at the cuffs, thread in the elastic to fit the doll and fasten off.

7 Work four evenly-spaced buttonloops on one edge of the back and sew the buttons into position.

Pinafore dress

The bodice

1 Backstitch all the shoulder seams to make two separate bodices [one bodice to form the lining]. Press open all the seams.

2 With the right sides together, backstitch along the neck and back edges of the bodice and the lining. Carefully snip both thicknesses of material at the corners.

3 Turn right side out and press.

4 Turn in the armhole edges of the bodice and the lining and oversew them together on the right side.

5 Join the two side seams on the wrong side of the material. Turn back to the right side and press.

The skirt

1 Cut one length of material 14cm × 45.5cm [5½in × 18in], and another length 11.5cm × 81cm [4½in × 32in].

2 Using running stitch, gather one edge of the longer piece and adjust it to fit the length of the shorter. With wrong sides together, join the two pieces of material with backstitch.

3 Press this seam towards the waist.

4 Pin the ribbon over the seam and hem both its edges to the material.

5 Join the centre back of the skirt with a french seam, leaving 13cm [5in] open at the top. Fold in these raw edges and hem them to make a neat opening.

6 Gather the top of the skirt to fit the bodice and, with the right sides together, leaving the lining loose, backstitch them along the gather line. Turn in the lining and hem it down to enclose the raw edges of the seam.

7 On one edge of the bodice make two buttonloops and sew the buttons into position.

8 Turn up and hem the skirt. Press.

Boots

1 Oversew the back and front seams and stitch the soles into position.
2 With a large darning needle pierce holes for the laces as indicated on your paper pattern.
3 Stitch in the tongues.
4 Ease the boots onto the doll, thread in the ribbons with a darning needle and tie.

GUARD'S UNIFORM

As illustrated on p. 27.

Materials required

Trousers
25cm of black poplin
One small red button
50cm of narrow red ribbon

Jacket
25cm of bright red poplin
Four small white buttons

Hat
Small piece of black fur fabric
25cm of narrow black ribbon
White feather

Boots
Small pieces of black leather

Belt
Narrow strip of white leather

Cutting out the pattern
Following the preparation instructions given on p. 22, cut out the pattern pieces.

Sewing
Sew 5mm [$\frac{3}{16}$ in] in from the raw edges.

Jacket

1 Backstitch all the shoulder and side seams to make two separate jackets [one jacket to form the lining]. Press open all the seams.
2 With the right sides together, backstitch the jacket and the lining to each other along the neck and centre front edges.

Turn to the right side and press.

3 Join the sleeves with french seams [see p. 21] and press them to one side.

4 Gather the top of the sleeves with running stitch to fit the jacket armholes, then backstitch to the jacket, leaving the jacket lining loose [see p. 21]. Turn inside out, tuck in the raw edges of the lining armholes and hem them down to enclose the raw edges of these seams.

5 Turn right side out.

6 Fold the raw edges of the jacket and lining hems to the inside and press them. Oversew the folded edges together.

7 Turn up and hem the cuffs.

8 Work four evenly-spaced buttonloops on one of the front edges and sew the buttons into position.

Trousers

1 Make a french seam down the centre back. Hem the centre fronts.

2 Make a french seam round the inside of the legs.

3 Pin the ribbon from waist to hem down the outside of the trouser legs, centering it on the side of each leg. Stitch it down along both its edges.

4 For the waistband, cut a 20mm [¾ in] wide strip of material on the bias to fit the doll.

5 Put the trousers on your doll and pin the front opening together at the waist. Make a deep vertical tuck at the waistband, each side of the opening, and each side of the back seam, to form 'creases' down the centre fronts and backs of each leg [see figure 42].

6 Remove the trousers from the doll and make a line of running stitch around the waist to hold the folded material in position.

7 With right sides together, backstitch the waistband to the trousers. Fold it over the raw edges of the seam. Turn up the raw edge of the waistband and hem it to the wrong side of the trousers along your original line of stitching.

8 Turn in the ends and oversew. Work a buttonloop on one end and sew a button onto the other.

9 Turn up and hem the legs.

10 Press centre creases down each leg.

Hat

1 On the wrong side of the fur fabric oversew the two halves together. Turn up a small hem along the brim and stitch it to the inside.

Fig 42

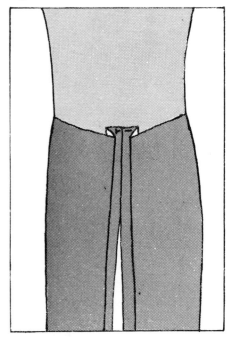

2 On one side seam sew a narrow ribbon to the inside of the hem. Try the hat on your doll so that you can see how long the ribbon must be, then fasten the loose end of the ribbon in place.

3 Position the feather and stitch it down.

Boots

1 With wrong sides together oversew the back and front edges on the right side.

2 Check that you have cut out both a left and a right sole and then sew them onto the boots.

3 With a large darning needle, make the holes for the laces as indicated on your paper pattern.

4 Sew the tongues into position.

5 Cut narrow leather laces. Ease the boots onto your doll, thread in the laces with a crochet hook and tie.

Belt

1 Cut a strip of white leather 7mm [¼in] wide to fit around your doll's waist, allowing an overlap of 25mm [1in].

2 Cut two pieces of white leather 13mm × 7mm [½in × ¼in] and oversew the narrow ends together to make two loops. Thread both loops onto one end of the belt. Place the belt on your doll and slip the other end through the loops to fasten it.

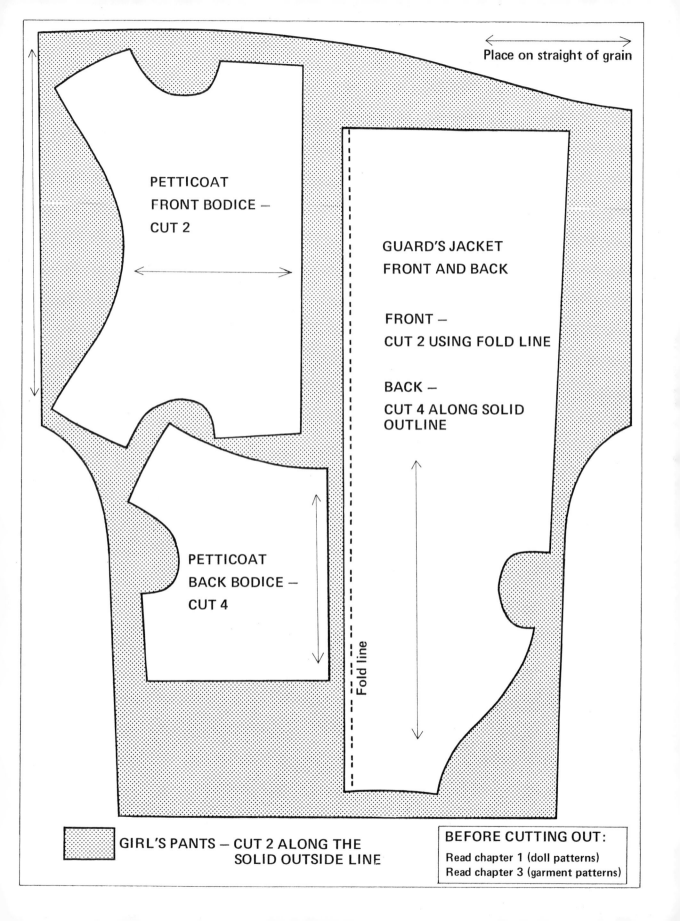

PETTICOAT
FRONT BODICE —
CUT 2

GUARD'S JACKET
FRONT AND BACK

FRONT —
CUT 2 USING FOLD LINE

BACK —
CUT 4 ALONG SOLID
OUTLINE

PETTICOAT
BACK BODICE —
CUT 4

Place on straight of grain

Fold line

GIRL'S PANTS — CUT 2 ALONG THE
SOLID OUTSIDE LINE

BEFORE CUTTING OUT:

Read chapter 1 (doll patterns)
Read chapter 3 (garment patterns)

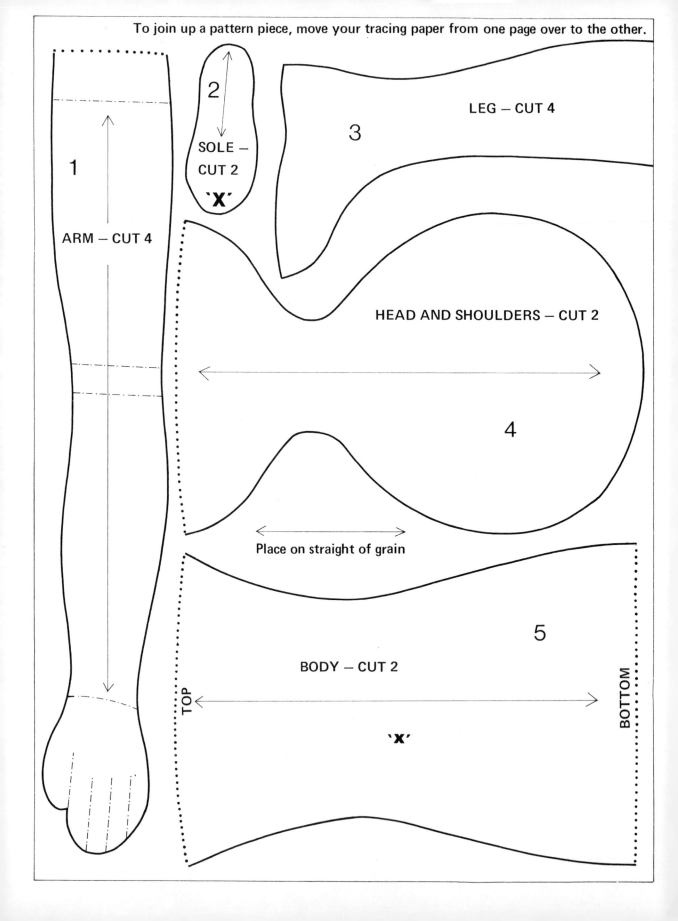

To join up a pattern piece, move your tracing paper from one page over to the other.

2

SOLE – CUT 2

'X'

3

LEG – CUT 4

1

ARM – CUT 4

HEAD AND SHOULDERS – CUT 2

4

Place on straight of grain

5

BODY – CUT 2

TOP

BOTTOM

'X'

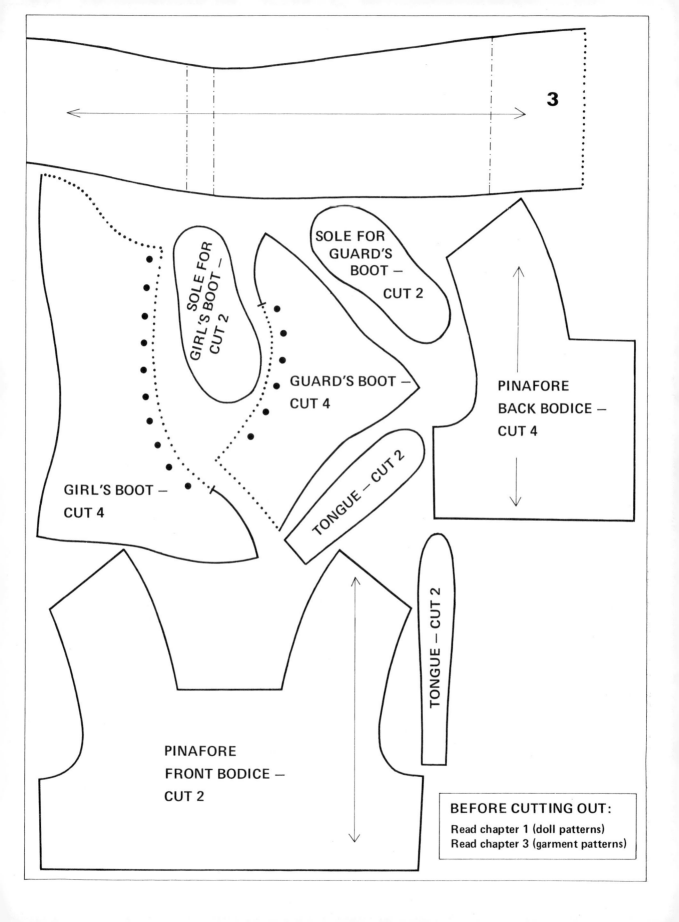

3

SOLE FOR GUARD'S BOOT — CUT 2

GIRL'S SOLE FOR BOOT — CUT 2

GUARD'S BOOT — CUT 4

GIRL'S BOOT — CUT 4

TONGUE — CUT 2

TONGUE — CUT 2

PINAFORE BACK BODICE — CUT 4

PINAFORE FRONT BODICE — CUT 2

BEFORE CUTTING OUT:

Read chapter 1 (doll patterns)
Read chapter 3 (garment patterns)

BEFORE CUTTING OUT:

Read chapter 1 (doll patterns)
Read chapter 3 (garment patterns)

Petticoat skirt: cut one length of material 25.5cm x 45.5cm [10in x 18in] and another 6.5cm x 76cm [2½in x 30in]

Pinafore skirt: cut one length of material 14cm x 45.5cm [5½in x 18in] and another 11.5cm x 81cm [4½in x 32in]

GUARD'S TROUSERS — CUT 2 ALONG THE SOLID OUTSIDE LINE

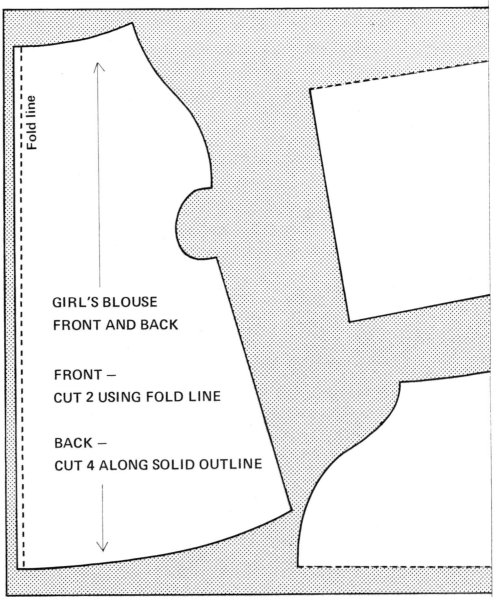

Fold line

GIRL'S BLOUSE
FRONT AND BACK

FRONT —
CUT 2 USING FOLD LINE

BACK —
CUT 4 ALONG SOLID OUTLINE

To join up a pattern piece, move your tracing paper from one page over to the other.

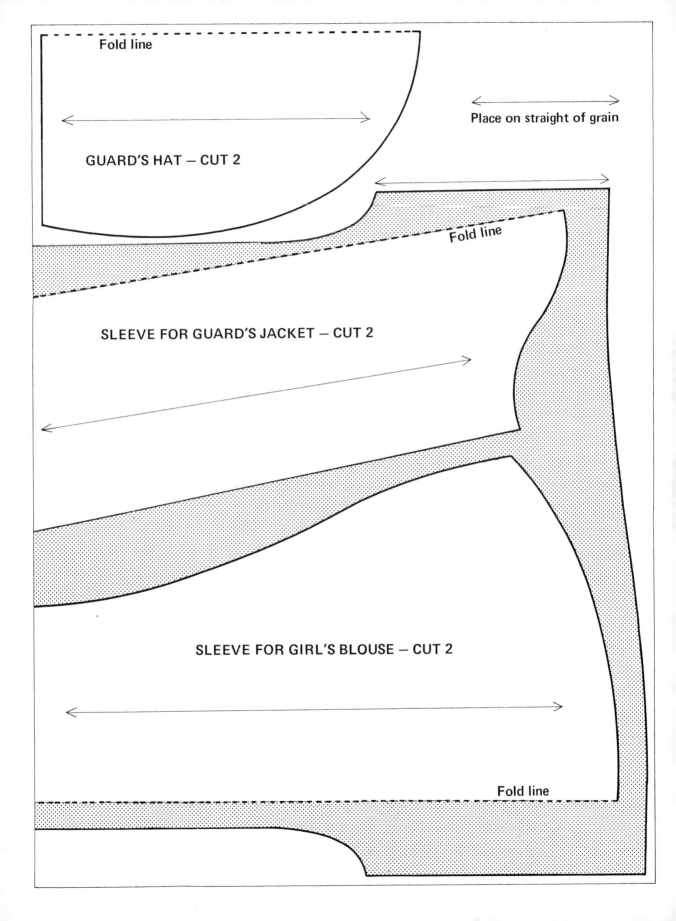

5. STICK DOLL

Height: 45cm [17¾in]
Two pattern pieces: 6 : 7

Materials required
25cm of unbleached calico
200g of 'Pure Airspanded Kapok'
Pale pink sewing thread
Yarn for the hair
Thread for the features
Blue, green or brown nail varnish for the eyes
Pink nail varnish for the lips and finger nails
A dowel 13mm [½in] in diameter, 43.5cm [17in] long
Leather for covering the stick

The idea for this doll came from the French 'Marottes' or, as they are sometimes called, 'Folly Head' dolls.

In the late 1870's a large number of these 'Marottes' were advertised in Paris by several manufacturers, the best known of whom were probably Rabery and Delphieu. This type of doll was also produced in Germany and was known there as a 'Schwenker'.

The originals consisted of a carved stick, at the end of which was a head wearing an ornate hat. A deep collar covered the mechanism of a musical box which played when the stick was turned. A few examples of this type of doll do have complete bodies with arms and legs and are dressed in elaborate costumes, but they are quite rare.

All the musical dolls were novelties and not really meant for children, so I have borrowed only the basic idea and have designed a doll which can be played with as a puppet.

Because these dolls are quick and easy to make, you could create a complete 'cast list' for a child who enjoys play acting, or help a group of children to make some for themselves.

This would also be a suitable doll to work on if you were interested in making historical costumes and characters.

Variations of the Stick Doll can be used to make characters for your own miniature theatre!

43

Opposite: Jointed Doll. See Chapter 6.

Cutting out the pattern
Following the preparation instructions given on p. 12, cut out the pattern pieces.

Sewing
With the right sides of the calico together, sew along your pencil lines with a small running stitch [see p. 11].
1 Join the two centre seams of the head and body.
2 Sew the two halves together.
3 Stitch round the arms, using backstitch when you reach the fingers and thumbs [see p. 8].
4 At the neck carefully make two or three snips on the edge of the material to ease the curve. Cut the material between the index finger and thumb on both hands.
5 Turn each piece right side out, using the blunt end of a crochet hook to ease the thumbs out, and whip the seams [see p. 11].

Stuffing
Before you begin this phase, read the general instructions on p. 14.

The arms
1 Place some kapok in the finger sections and work it well up to the seam lines.
2 With stabbing stitch [see p. 11] work the three lines on each hand as marked on your paper pattern to create the individual fingers.
3 Place more kapok in the palms and, using the crochet hook, stuff it firmly into each thumb.
4 With a small running stitch sew along the inside wrist lines as indicated on your paper pattern, from one seam to the other, slightly gathering the material. Fasten off the thread securely.
5 Keeping the shape smooth and firm, continue stuffing up to the elbows.
6 Take one of the arms, join the thread at one of the side seams directly above the stuffing and make a line of stabbing stitch across the top of the stuffing, from seam to seam [see figure 43].
7 Continue stuffing to within 25mm [1in] of the opening, then make another line of stabbing stitch as before.
8 Turn in the raw edges 5mm [$\frac{3}{16}$ in] at the opening and oversew them together.
9 Finish the other arm in the same way.

Fig 43

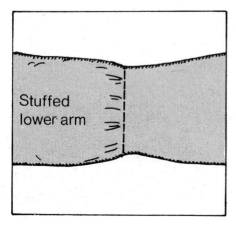

Stuffed lower arm

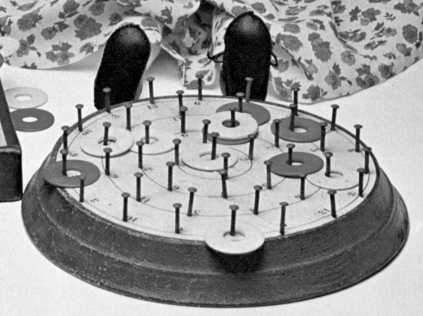

The head and body

1 Stuff the head firmly to just above the neck.
2 Push the stick up into the head, by slowly twisting it round, as far as it will go.
3 With the crochet hook stuff the neck with really small pieces of kapok until it is firm and straight.
4 Keeping the stick in the centre of your doll, continue to stuff the body around it.
5 Turn in the raw edge, pulling the material tightly around the stick, and oversew the front and back together from side seam to side seam.
6 Stitch the top seams of the arms to the shoulders of the body [see figure 44].

The stick

1 Cut a length of leather to cover the stick. Hold it in position over the stick and oversew the side seam.
2 Stitch the top edge of the leather to your doll.
3 Cut a circle of leather to fit the bottom of the stick and oversew it to the bottom edge of the leather already in place.

Bringing your doll to life

Following the instructions given in Chapter Two, work the face and hair.

Paint the tips of each finger and thumb with pink nail varnish.

Dressing your doll

I have supplied only the basic bodice and sleeve patterns because these are all that you will require to produce different dresses.

Fig 44

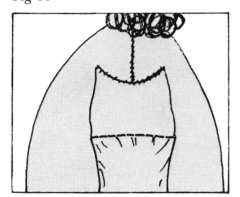

Opposite: Sally Ann. See Chapter 6.

As the head and torso sections are cut together the face must be worked after construction has been completed.

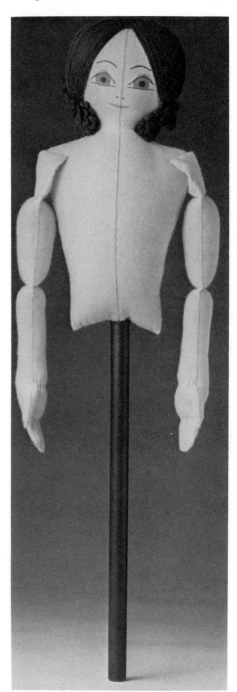

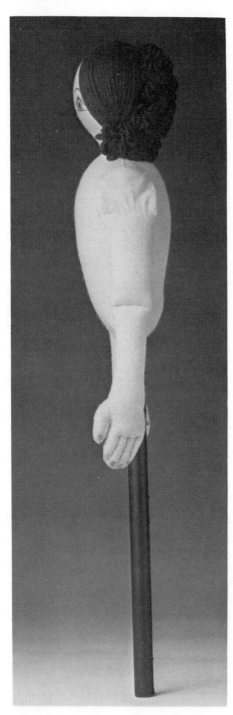

The shaping of the torso gives a natural look to the Stick Doll when it is dressed.

If you raise or lower the neck line, be sure to retain the angle of the shoulders. You can change the style of the sleeves in any way you choose provided that you use the armhole shape given on the pattern.

Long petticoat and dress
As illustrated on p. 28.

Materials required

Petticoat	Dress
40cm of white lawn	20cm of plain fabric
Three small white buttons	60cm of patterned fabric
1m of narrow white lace	Three small buttons

Cutting out the pattern
Following the preparation instructions given on p. 22, cut out the pattern pieces.

Sewing
Sew 5mm [$\frac{3}{16}$ in] in from the raw edges.

Petticoat

The bodice
1 Backstitch all the shoulder and side seams, to make two separate bodices [one bodice to form the lining].
2 Press open all the seams.
3 With the right sides together, join along the necks and centre backs with a small running stitch. Turn the bodice right side out and press.
4 Cut a strip of material on the bias 13mm [½in] wide, press in the side edges and use it to bind the armholes.

The skirt
1 Cut a length of material 24cm × 56cm [9in × 24in].
2 Join the centre back with a french seam [see p. 21], leaving a 12.5cm [5in] opening at the top.
3 Turn in and hem these edges.
4 With a small running stitch gather the top of the skirt to fit the bodice and backstitch it to the bodice, leaving the bodice lining loose [see p. 22]. Turn in the raw edge of the lining and hem it down to enclose the raw edges of this seam.
5 Work three evenly-spaced buttonloops on one edge of the back bodice and sew the buttons into position.
6 Turn up and hem the skirt. Stitch the lace to the bottom of the hem, edge to edge, and press.

Dress

The bodice

1 Backstitch all the shoulder and side seams to make two separate bodices [one bodice to form the lining]. Press open all the seams.
2 With the right sides together, join the bodices with a small running stitch along the neck and back edges.
3 Turn right side out and press.
4 Use french seams to join up the sleeves. Press them to one side.
5 With a small running stitch gather the tops of the sleeves to fit the bodice armholes, then backstitch them to the bodice, leaving the bodice lining loose [see p. 21].
6 Turn in the armhole edges of the lining and hem them down to enclose the raw edges.
7 Turn up and hem the cuffs.

The skirt

1 Cut a length of material 29cm × 92cm [11½in × 36in].
2 French seam the centre back join to within 12.5cm [5in] of the top. Turn in and hem the remaining raw edges to make a neat opening.
3 Using a running stitch, gather the top of the skirt to fit the bodice and backstitch it to the bodice, leaving the bodice lining loose.
4 Turn in the raw edge of the lining and hem it down to enclose the raw edges of this join.
5 Work three evenly-spaced buttonloops on one edge of the back bodice, and sew on the buttons.
6 Turn up and hem the skirt. Press.

It is important to allow the arms to hang freely when attaching them to the shoulders.

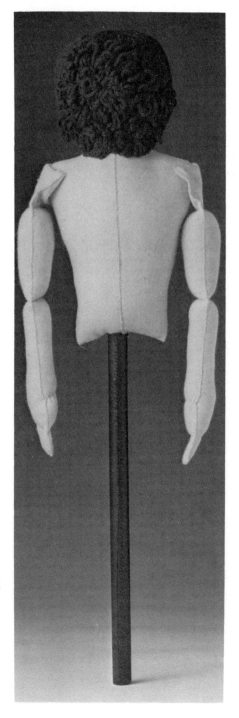

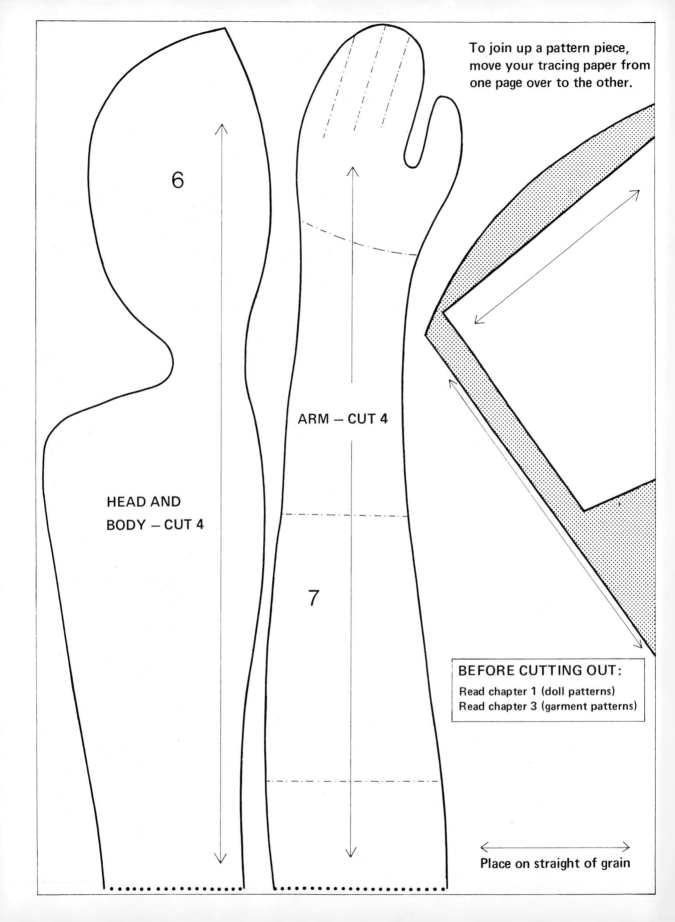

To join up a pattern piece, move your tracing paper from one page over to the other.

6

ARM — CUT 4

HEAD AND
BODY — CUT 4

7

BEFORE CUTTING OUT:

Read chapter 1 (doll patterns)
Read chapter 3 (garment patterns)

Place on straight of grain

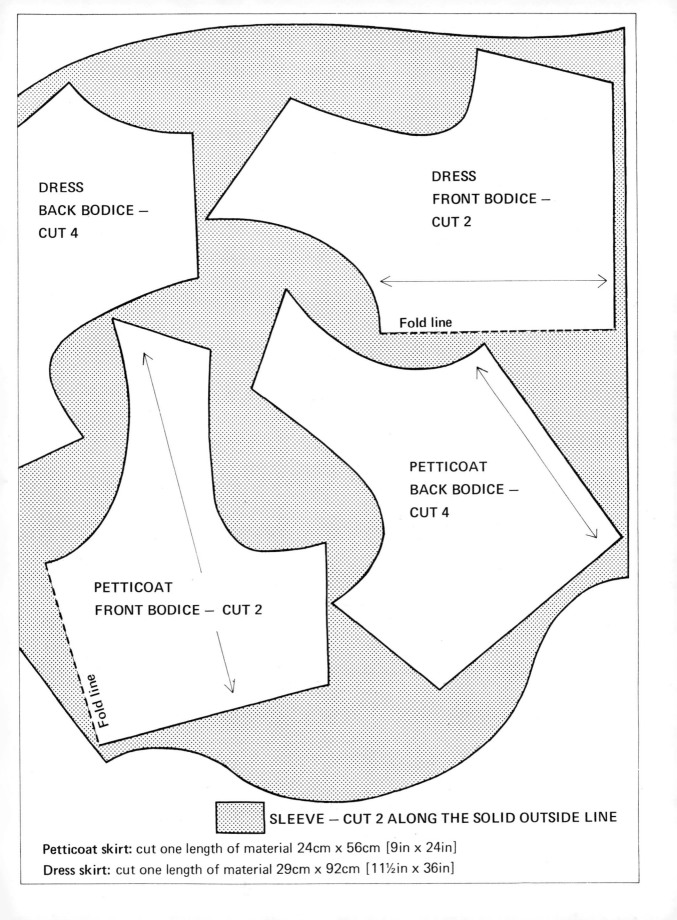

DRESS
BACK BODICE —
CUT 4

DRESS
FRONT BODICE —
CUT 2

Fold line

PETTICOAT
BACK BODICE —
CUT 4

PETTICOAT
FRONT BODICE — CUT 2

Fold line

SLEEVE — CUT 2 ALONG THE SOLID OUTSIDE LINE

Petticoat skirt: cut one length of material 24cm x 56cm [9in x 24in]

Dress skirt: cut one length of material 29cm x 92cm [11½in x 36in]

6. JOINTED DOLL

Height: 45.5cm [18in]
Eight pattern pieces: 8 : 9 : 10 : 11 : 12 : 13 : 14 : 15

Materials required
40cm of unbleached calico
250g of 'Pure Airspanded Kapok'
Pale pink sewing thread
50cm of 5mm elastic
Four strong, shanked buttons, line 24 [⅝in]
Yarn for the hair
Thread for the features
Blue, green or brown nail varnish for the eyes
Pale pink nail varnish for the lips and finger nails

For this doll I have gone back to the early method of joining
arms and legs to the body with elastic fastened to strong,
shanked buttons. This type of construction, which enables each
limb to be turned separately, full circle, adapts well to a cloth
doll.

You will find the jointed doll provides an ideal basis for boy and
toddler characters because the bent limbs give a lifelike and
alert appearance. If, however, your doll is for a very young
child, who might be excessively rough with it, straighten the
arms and legs so that the angles at the knees and elbows are not
too great. The reason for this is that if one of the bent limbs is
held like a wishbone and pulled hard, it will tear!

To alter the knee and elbow angles, trace round the bottom half
of the pattern, then—keeping the knee or elbow in position—
turn the pattern to the angle you require. Now complete the
tracing.

A more 'babylike' doll can be made by thickening the limbs
from the wrists and ankles upwards; this will give you a
chubbier effect.

Cutting out the pattern
Following the preparation instructions given on p. 12, cut out
the pattern pieces.

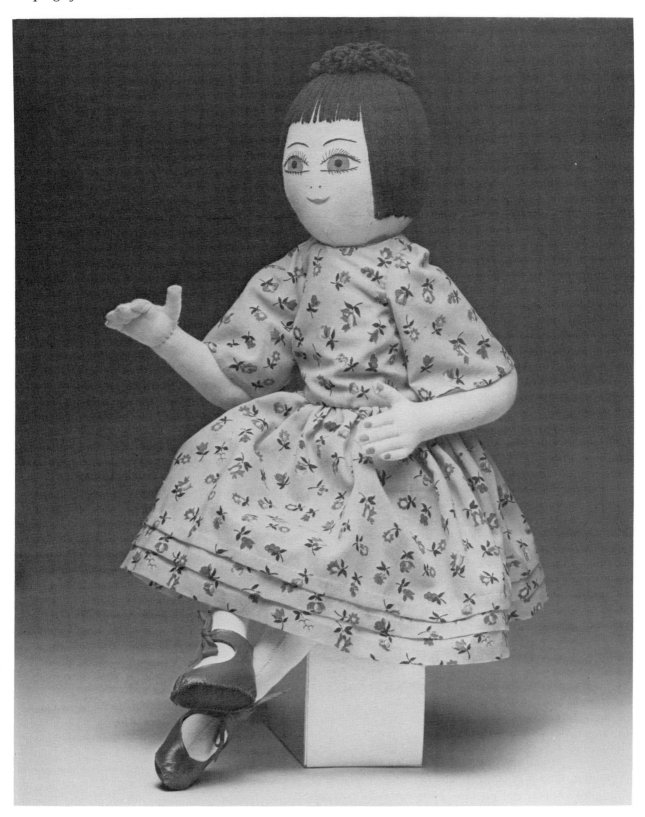

Sewing

With the right sides of the calico together, sew along your pencil lines with a small running stitch [see p. 11].

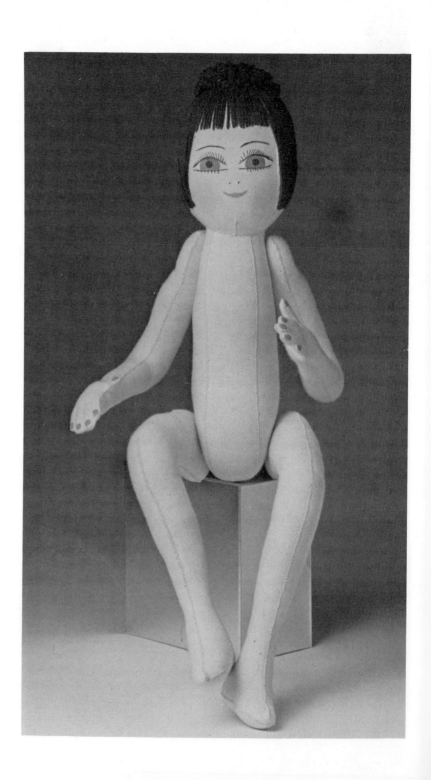

The body
Join the body gusset to the two side sections, and stitch the darts.

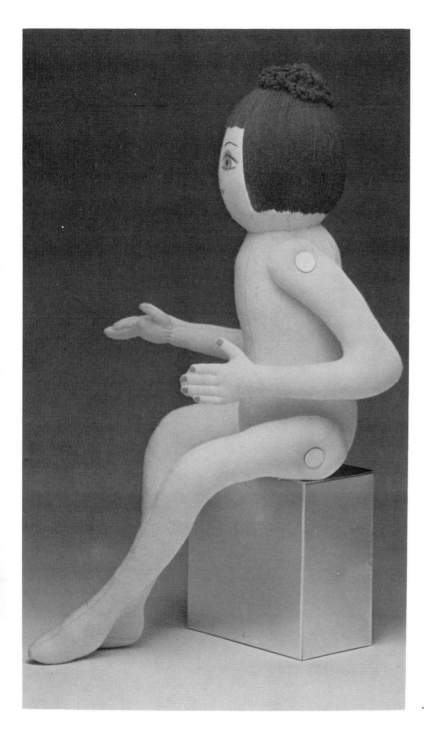

The neat and simple method of attaching the limbs gives the Jointed Doll lots of mobility.

The legs

1 Starting at the bottom of the opening, sew down the backs of the legs.
2 From the other end of the opening sew round the tops and down the fronts.
3 Making sure that you have a left and a right sole, stitch them into position.

The arms

1 From one end of the opening sew round the arms, using backstitch [see p. 8] for the finger and thumb sections.
2 Carefully make two or three snips on the edge of the material between the index finger and the thumb on each hand.

The head

1 Stitch the darts and join the four pieces. Turn all the parts right side out, using the blunt end of a crochet hook to ease out the thumbs, and whip the seams [see p. 11].

Stuffing

Before you begin this phase, read the general instructions on p. 14.

The legs

1 Stuff the feet and legs up to the bottom of the openings.
2 Now stuff the tops of the legs. Make sure that the rounded shape along the seams is firm, but do not stuff the tops too tightly—they should give when pressed firmly between your index finger and thumb.
3 Complete the stuffing. Turn in the raw edges and oversew [see p. 11] the openings neatly.

Fig 45

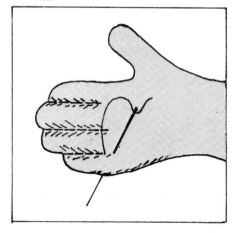

The arms

1 Place a little kapok in the hands and work it well up to the finger seams.
2 Using a stabbing stitch [see p. 11] sew the three lines on each hand to make the individual fingers [see figure 45], following the markings on your paper pattern.
3 Place more kapok in the palms and use the crochet hook to stuff it firmly into each thumb.
4 With a small running stitch sew along the inside wrist lines, as indicated on your paper pattern, from one seam to the other, slightly gathering the material. Fasten off the thread securely.
5 Finish stuffing the arms as you did the legs and oversew the openings.

The body

1 Stuff the body firmly but not too tightly up to the waist.
2 Thread a 20.5cm [8in] length of elastic through the shank of a button. With the crochet hook make a hole, as shown on your paper pattern, through one of the legs. Pull the two ends of the elastic through.
3 Checking that you have the left and right legs the correct way round, take the elastic through the body and the second leg [see figure 46].
4 Thread one of the ends of the elastic through another button and pull the three sections [the legs and the body] together as tightly as possible. Knot the elastic several times and cut off the excess.
5 Continue to stuff the body firmly to within 25mm [1in] of the opening.
6 Fasten the arms onto the body as for the legs.
7 Continue stuffing as tightly as possible, right up to the opening.

The head

Stuff the head carefully, watching all the time to see that the face surface remains smooth.

Bringing your doll to life

1 Following the instructions given in Chapter Two, work the face.
2 Hold the head onto the body at the most attractive angle. Tuck in the raw edges of the head and stitch it firmly to the body by sewing along the join several times until there are no visible gaps [see figure 47].
3 To make the hair, follow the instructions given in Chapter Two.
4 Finish the doll by painting the tips of each finger and thumb with pink nail varnish.

Dressing your doll

From the following patterns you will be able to create a variety of outfits, merely by altering the lengths of skirts, sleeves and trousers.

Because this doll's body is wider from back to front than from side to side, the bodice patterns are cut in one piece, to achieve a really good fit.

Fig 46

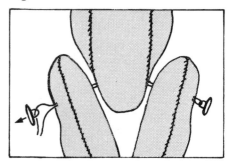

Fig 47

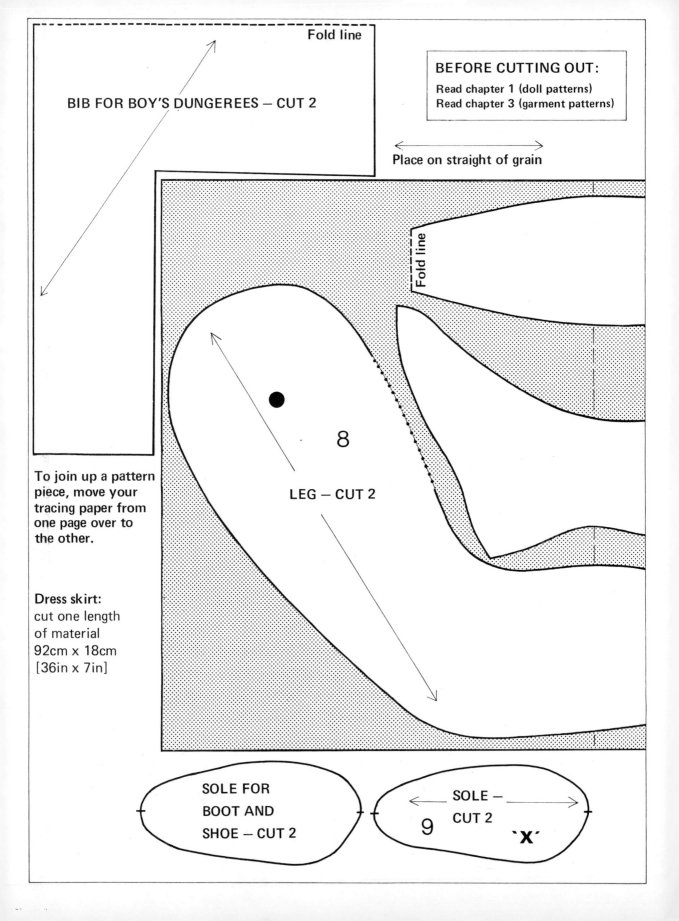

Fold line

BIB FOR BOY'S DUNGEREES – CUT 2

BEFORE CUTTING OUT:

Read chapter 1 (doll patterns)
Read chapter 3 (garment patterns)

Place on straight of grain

Fold line

8

LEG – CUT 2

To join up a pattern piece, move your tracing paper from one page over to the other.

Dress skirt:
cut one length of material
92cm x 18cm
[36in x 7in]

SOLE FOR BOOT AND SHOE – CUT 2

SOLE – CUT 2

9

`X´

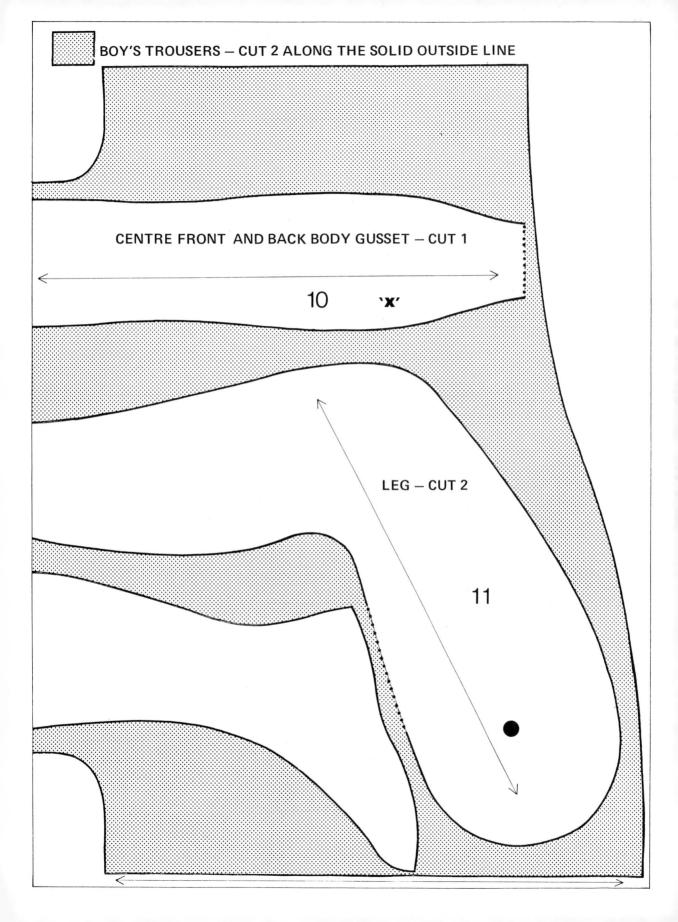

BOY'S TROUSERS – CUT 2 ALONG THE SOLID OUTSIDE LINE

CENTRE FRONT AND BACK BODY GUSSET – CUT 1

10   'x'

LEG – CUT 2

11

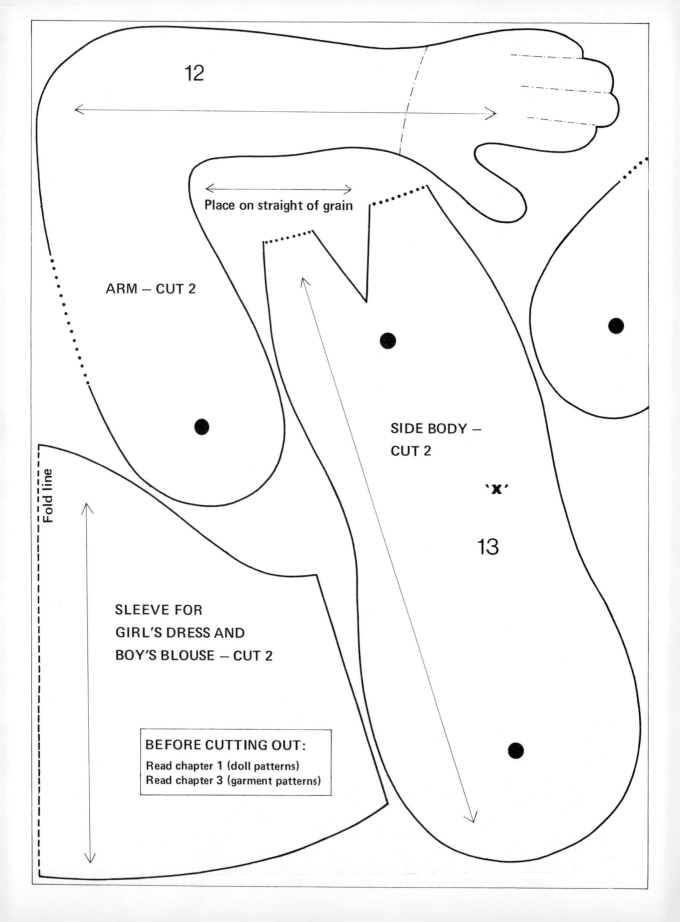

12

ARM – CUT 2

Place on straight of grain

SIDE BODY –
CUT 2

'x'

13

Fold line

SLEEVE FOR
GIRL'S DRESS AND
BOY'S BLOUSE – CUT 2

BEFORE CUTTING OUT:

Read chapter 1 (doll patterns)
Read chapter 3 (garment patterns)

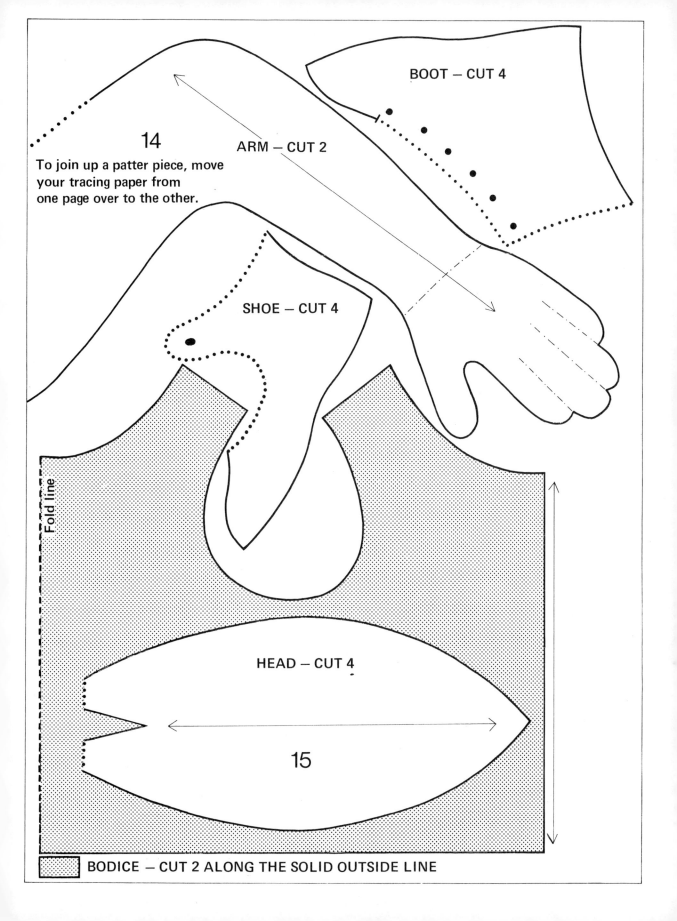

BOOT – CUT 4

14

ARM – CUT 2

To join up a patter piece, move
your tracing paper from
one page over to the other.

SHOE – CUT 4

Fold line

HEAD – CUT 4

15

BODICE – CUT 2 ALONG THE SOLID OUTSIDE LINE

GIRL'S OUTFIT

As illustrated on p. 45.

Materials required

Matching dress and pants
50cm of printed lawn
Three small buttons
50cm of 5mm elastic

Shoes
Small pieces of red and black leather
50cm of narrow red ribbon

Cutting out the pattern
Following the preparation instructions given on p. 22, cut out the pattern pieces.

Sewing
Sew 5mm [$\frac{3}{16}$ in] in from the raw edges.

Dress

The bodice
1 Backstitch all the shoulder seams to make two separate bodices [one bodice to form the lining]. Press open all the seams.
2 With the right sides together join the bodices along the neck and back edges with a small running stitch.
3 Turn right side out and press.

The sleeves
1 Use a french seam to join the sleeves [see p. 21]. Turn up and hem the cuffs. Press.
2 Gather the tops of the sleeves with a small running stitch to fit the bodice armholes, and backstitch them to the bodice leaving the bodice lining loose [see p. 21].
3 Turn in the armhole edges of the lining and hem them down to enclose the raw edges of the seams.

Opposite: Victorian Dolls. See Chapter 8.

The skirt

1 Cut a length of material 92cm × 18cm [36in × 7in].
2 Join the centre back with a french seam, leaving 7.5cm [3in] open at the top [see p. 21]. Turn in and hem down these raw edges to make a neat opening.
3 With a running stitch gather the top of the skirt to fit the bodice, then backstitch it to the bodice, leaving the bodice lining loose [see p. 22].
4 Turn in the raw edge of the lining and hem it down to enclose the raw edges of this seam.
5 Work three evenly-spaced buttonloops [see p. 22] on one edge of the back bodice and sew on the buttons.
6 Turn up and hem the skirt.
7 Just above the hem on the right side make two tucks [see figure 48] with running stitch. Press the tucks towards the hem.

Pants

1 Make french seams down the centre back and front of the pants and press them to one side.
2 Join the inside legs with a french seam.
3 Leaving openings for the elastic, make a 7mm [¼in] hem round both the waist and the legs.
4 Thread in the elastic, adjust it to fit the doll and then fasten it off securely.

Shoes

1 Oversew the front and back seams.
2 Check that you have a left and a right sole, then stitch them into position.
3 Use a large darning needle to make the holes for the laces as indicated on your paper pattern.
4 Fit the shoes onto your doll, thread in the ribbons and tie.

Fig 48

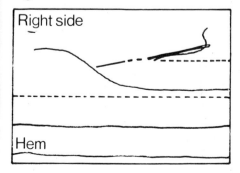

Right side

Hem

BOY'S OUTFIT

As illustrated on p. 45.

Materials required

Blouse
25cm of printed lawn
Four small matching buttons
25cm of 5mm elastic

Dungarees
25cm of plain poplin
Three small matching buttons

Boots
Small pieces of black leather

Cutting out the pattern
Following the preparation instructions given on p. 22, cut out the pattern pieces.

Sewing
Sew 5mm [$\frac{3}{16}$ in] in from the raw edges.

Blouse
The bodice
1 Backstitch all the shoulder seams to make two separate bodices [one bodice to form the lining]. Press open all the seams.
2 Right sides together, join them with a small running stitch along the neck and back edges.
3 Turn right side out and press.

The sleeves
1 Join up the sleeves with french seams.
2 Gather the tops of the sleeves with a small running stitch until they fit the bodice armholes, then backstitch them to the bodice, leaving the bodice lining loose [see p. 21].
3 Turn in the armhole edges of the lining and hem them down to enclose the raw edges of these seams.
4 Make a 7mm [¼in] hem on each cuff and thread the elastic through to fit your doll.
5 Turn in the bottom edges of the bodice and neatly oversew them together. Press.

Dungarees

The bib

1 Right sides together, backstitch round the top edges [see figure 49].
2 Snip the edge of the material at the corners, turn right side out and press.

The trousers

1 Use french seams to join the centre front and 7.5cm [3in] at the bottom of the centre back.
2 Turn in the remainder of these edges and hem them down to make a neat opening [see p. 21].
3 Join the inside legs with a french seam.
4 With a running stitch gather the top of the trousers to fit the waistband of the bib, then backstitch it to the bib, leaving the bib lining loose [see p. 22].
5 Turn in and hem down the lining to enclose the raw edges of this seam.
6 Fold the material at the bottom of the legs to make the turn-ups, then hem them down [see figure 50].

The braces

1 Cut two strips of material 14cm × 2cm [5½in × ¾in]. Turn in the raw edges and hem round them.
2 Work a buttonloop [see p. 22] at one end of each strip and sew the other ends to the inside of the waistband at the back to cross one another.
3 Sew two buttons on the bib, one at each corner.
4 Make another buttonloop on one end of the waistband and sew a button to the other. Press.

Boots

1 Oversew the front and back seams.
2 Making sure that you have the soles the right way round, stitch them into place.
3 With a large darning needle, pierce the holes for the laces as marked on your paper pattern.
4 Sew in the tongues.
5 Cut narrow strips of leather for the laces.
6 Fit the boots onto your doll, thread in the laces using a crochet hook, and tie.

Fig 49

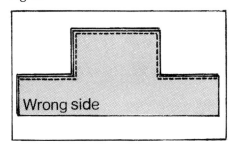

Wrong side

Fig 50

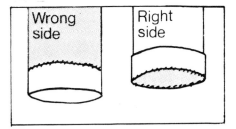

Wrong side   Right side

7. SALLY ANN

Height: 40.5cm [16in]
Nine pattern pieces: 16 : 17 : 18 : 19 : 20 : 21 : 22 : 23 : 24

Materials required
30cm of unbleached calico
200g of 'Pure Airspanded Kapok'
Pale pink sewing thread
Yarn for the hair
Thread for the features
Blue, green or brown nail varnish for the eyes
Pink nail varnish for the lips and finger nails

Whenever I make this doll it always turns out to be a cheeky young girl with a distinctive character and, however hard I try to resist, she inevitably ends up smiling. Perhaps you will have more control over her!
Like many of the old dolls, this one is impossible to categorise and so I have just called her Sally Ann.

If you make this doll for a child in the 'destructive' age group, straighten the arms as described for the jointed doll in the previous chapter. Be careful when you are sewing the legs that you have a left and a right — it is quite easy to get muddled and end up with two identical legs.

Cutting out the pattern
Following the preparation instructions given on p. 12, cut out the pattern pieces.

Sewing
With the right sides of the calico together, sew along your pencil lines with a small running stitch [see p. 11].
1 Starting with the body, join the centre back seam.
2 Leaving the neck open, stitch the front and back sections together.
3 Sew round the arms, using backstitch [see p. 8] for the hands.
4 Pin the inside and outside leg sections together so that you have a left and a right, then stitch the front and the back seams.

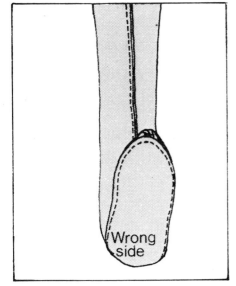

Fig 52

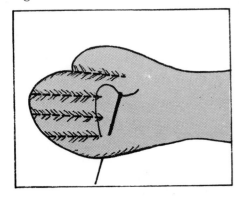

5 Stitch the soles into position the correct way round [see figure 51], bearing in mind that the legs are inside out.

6 Join together the five head sections.

7 Turn each piece right side out and whip the seams [see p. 11].

Stuffing

Before you begin this phase, read the general instructions on p. 14.

see p. 14.

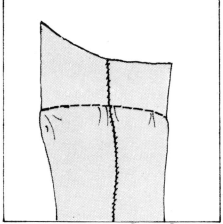

Fig 53

The arms

1 Place a small amount of kapok in the hands and work it well up to the finger seams.

2 Using a stabbing stitch [see p. 11] sew the four lines on each hand to make the individual fingers and thumbs [see figure 52] following the markings on your paper pattern.

3 Place more kapok in the palms.

4 With a small running stitch, sew along the inside wrist lines as indicated on your paper pattern, from one seam to the other, slightly gathering the material. Fasten the thread off securely.

5 Stuff the rest of the arms to within 13mm [½ in] of the opening.

6 Turn in the raw edges 5mm [$\frac{3}{16}$ in] and oversew the opening.

Fig 54

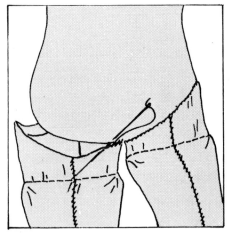

The legs

1 Keeping the seams straight, stuff the feet and legs up to the lines indicated on your paper pattern.

2 Sew across these lines with stabbing stitch [see figure 53].

The body

1 Stuff the body as firmly as you can, right up to the neck opening. The kapok should, in fact, protrude slightly from the opening.

2 Turn in the top raw edges of the legs 5mm [$\frac{3}{16}$ in] and tack round them with long running stitches.

3 Pin the leg openings to the body [see figure 54] and stitch them on securely.

4 Sew the tops of the arms to the shoulders of the body along the oversewn lines and then 7mm [¼ in] down from these lines [see figure 55].

Fig 55

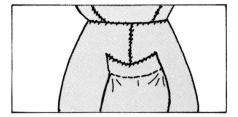

The head

Keeping the front and side surfaces smooth, stuff the head. Push the cheeks out evenly or else your doll will look as though she has toothache!

Bringing your doll to life

1 Following the instructions given in Chapter Two, work the face.
2 Hold the head onto the body at the most attractive angle. Tuck in the raw edges and stitch them together by sewing along the join several times until there are no visible gaps.
3 Make the hair, following the instructions given in Chapter Two.
4 Add the finishing touches by carefully painting the tips of the fingers and thumb with pink nail varnish.

Dressing your doll

Sally Ann's full-skirted dress has long sleeves but short sleeves suit her just as well. Under the dress are long bloomers and a waist petticoat.

SALLY ANN'S OUTFIT

As illustrated on p. 46.

Materials required

Petticoat and bloomers
50cm of white lawn
50cm of 5mm elastic
120cm of narrow white lace

Dress
50cm of printed voile
1m of narrow ribbon

Shoes
Small pieces of leather or suede

Cutting out the pattern
Following the preparation instructions given on p. 22, cut out the pattern pieces.

Sewing
Sew 5mm [$\frac{3}{16}$ in] in from the raw edges.

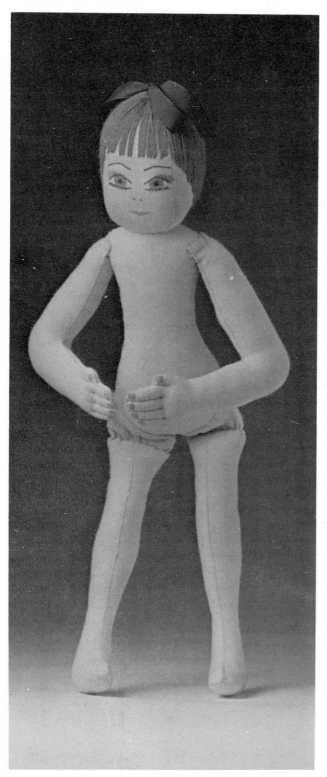
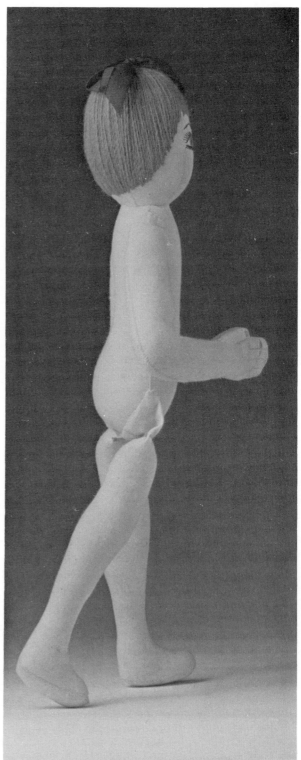

When Sally Ann is undressed, she is shapely and elegant.

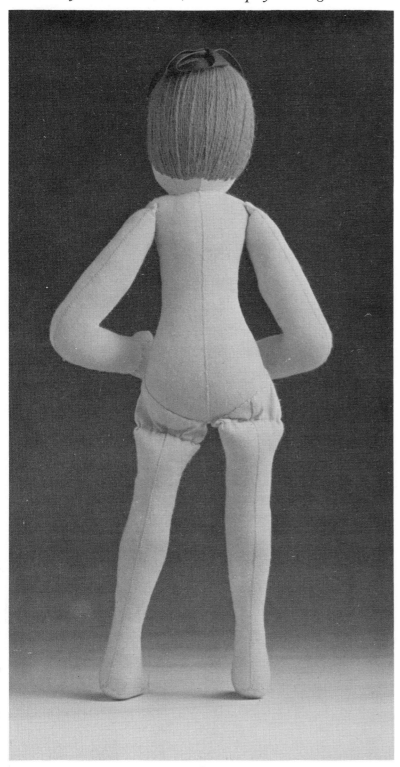

Petticoat

1 Cut a length of material 20.5cm × 92cm [8in × 36in] and join the centre back with a french seam [see p. 21].
2 Leaving an opening for the elastic, make a 7mm [¼in] hem along one edge. Thread in the elastic to fit your doll's waist and fasten it securely.
3 Turn up and hem the other edge. Press and stitch the lace to the bottom of the hem, edge to edge.

Bloomers

1 Use french seams to join the centre front and back edges. Press these to one side.
2 Join the inside legs in the same way.
3 Leaving openings for the elastic, make a 7mm [¼in] hem along the waist and leg edges.
4 Stitch the lace to the bottom of the leg hems, edge to edge.
5 Thread in the elastic at the waist and legs to fit your doll, then fasten off.

Dress

The bodice

1 Backstitch all the shoulder and side seams to make two separate bodices [one bodice to form the lining]. Press open all the seams.
2 With the right sides together, join the two sections along the neck and back edges.
3 Turn right side out and press.

The sleeves

1 Join with french seams. Press the seams to one side.
2 With a small running stitch gather the tops of the sleeves to fit the armholes of the bodice. Backstitch them to the bodice, leaving the bodice lining loose [see p. 21].
3 Turn in the armhole edges of the lining and hem them down to enclose the raw edges of the seams.
4 Make a 7mm [¼in] hem on each cuff and thread in the elastic to fit your doll's wrists.

The skirt

1 Cut a length of material 20.5cm × 92cm [8in × 36in] and join the centre back with a french seam, leaving 7.5cm [3in] open at the waist [see p. 21].
2 Turn in these raw edges and hem them down to make a neat opening.
3 With a small running stitch gather the top of the skirt to fit the bodice and backstitch it to the bodice, leaving the bodice lining loose [see p. 22].

4 Turn in the lining and hem it down to enclose the raw edges of this seam.

5 Work three evenly-spaced buttonloops on one edge of the back bodice [see p. 22], and sew the buttons into position.

6 Turn up and hem the skirt. Press.

7 Dress your doll and tie the ribbon around her waist.

Shoes

1 Oversew the front and back seams.

2 Making sure that you have a left and a right sole, sew them into place.

3 Use a large darning needle to pierce the holes for the laces as indicated on your paper pattern.

5 Cut two thin strips of leather for the laces.

6 Ease the shoes onto your doll, thread in the laces with a crochet hook, and tie.

Petticoat: cut one length of material
20.5cm x 92cm [8in x 36in]

Dress skirt: cut one length of material
20.5cm x 92cm [8in x 36in]

BEFORE CUTTING OUT:

Read chapter 1 (doll patterns)
Read chapter 3 (garment patterns)

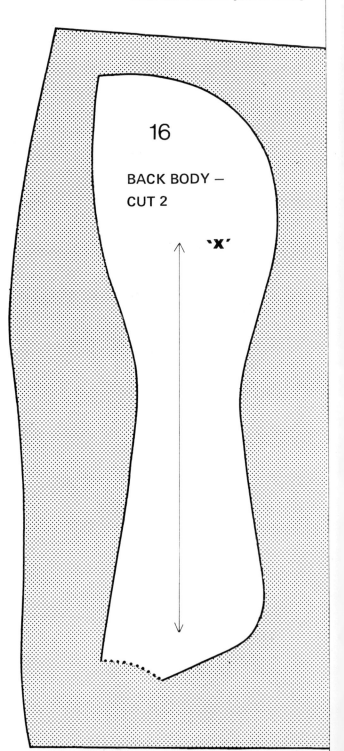

16

BACK BODY —
CUT 2

'x'

Place on straight of grain

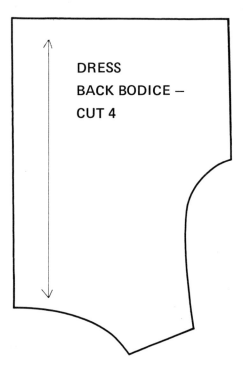

DRESS
BACK BODICE —
CUT 4

To join up a pattern piece, move your tracing paper from one page over to the other.

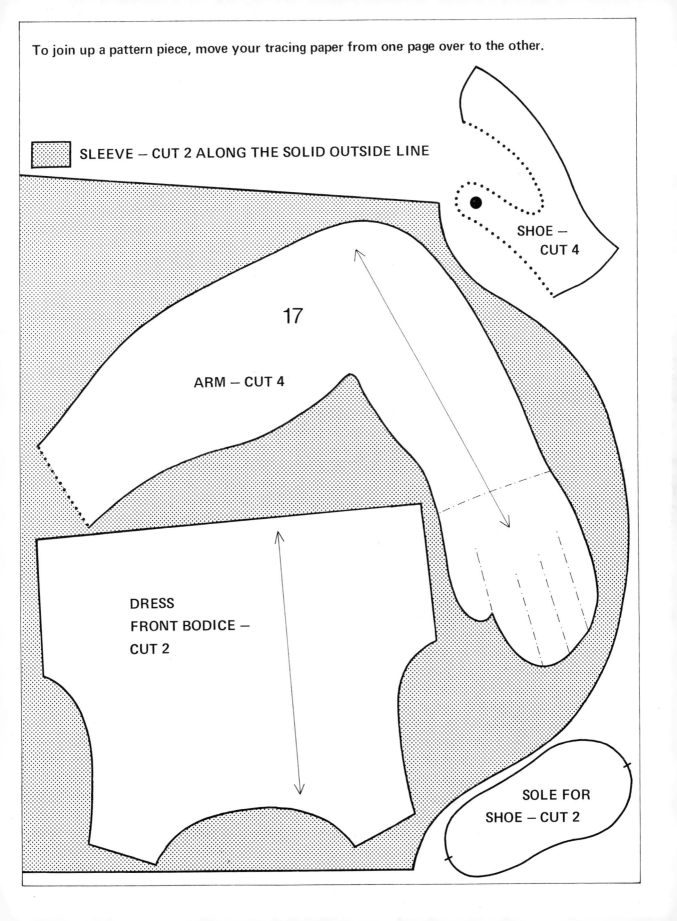

SLEEVE — CUT 2 ALONG THE SOLID OUTSIDE LINE

SHOE — CUT 4

17

ARM — CUT 4

DRESS
FRONT BODICE —
CUT 2

SOLE FOR
SHOE — CUT 2

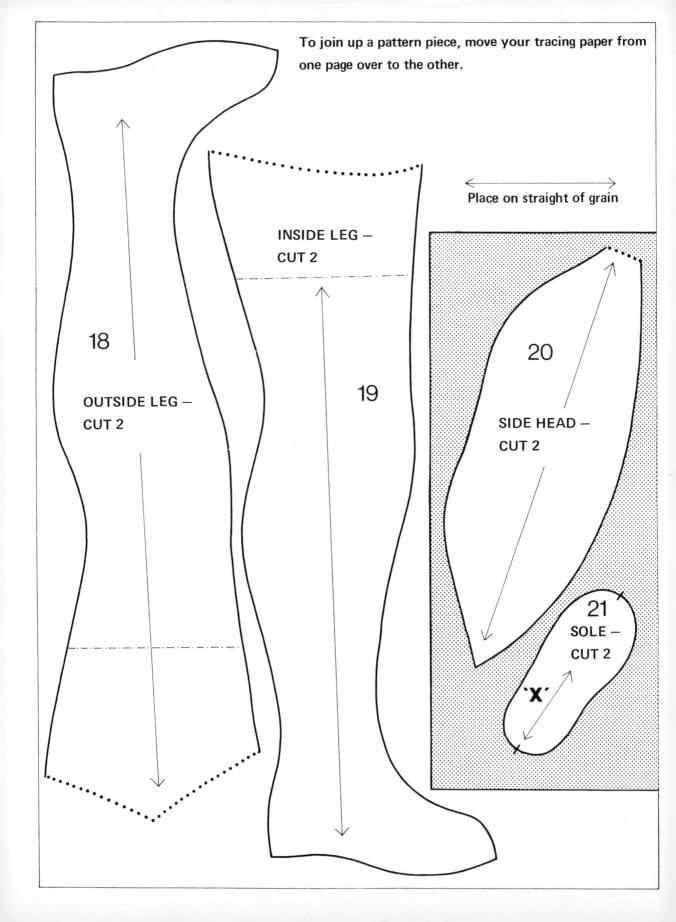

To join up a pattern piece, move your tracing paper from one page over to the other.

Place on straight of grain

INSIDE LEG – CUT 2

18

OUTSIDE LEG – CUT 2

19

20

SIDE HEAD – CUT 2

21

SOLE – CUT 2

'X'

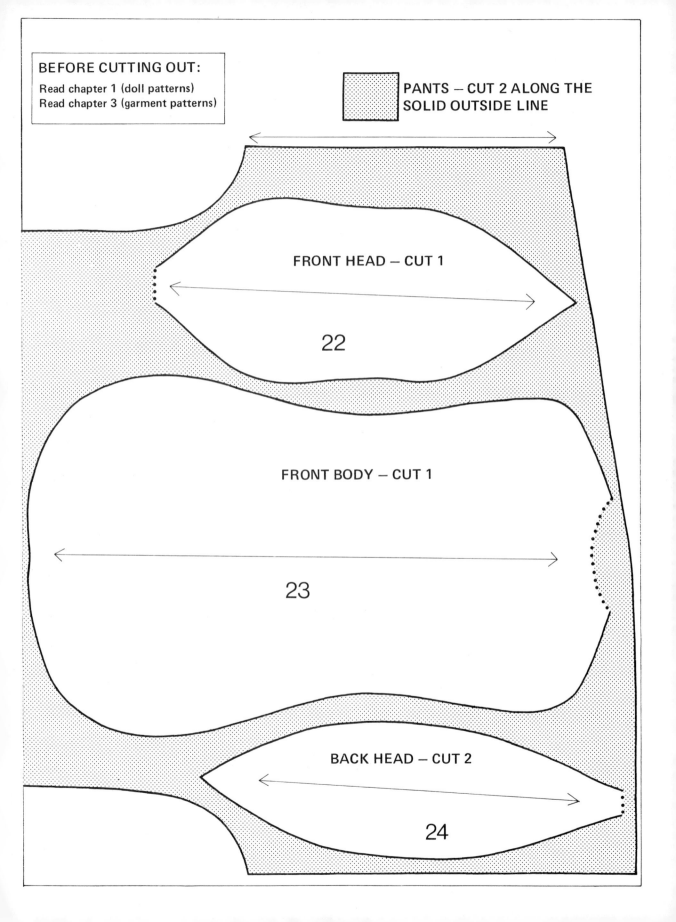

BEFORE CUTTING OUT:

Read chapter 1 (doll patterns)
Read chapter 3 (garment patterns)

PANTS — CUT 2 ALONG THE
SOLID OUTSIDE LINE

FRONT HEAD — CUT 1

22

FRONT BODY — CUT 1

23

BACK HEAD — CUT 2

24

8. VICTORIAN DOLL

Height: 60.5cm [23¾ in]
Twelve pattern pieces:
25 : 26 : 27 : 28 : 29 : 30 : 31 : 32 : 33 : 34 : 35 : 36

Materials required

60cm of unbleached calico

400g of 'Pure Airspanded Kapok'

Pale pink sewing thread

Yarn for the hair

Thread for the features

Blue, green or brown nail varnish for the eyes

Pink nail varnish for the lips and finger nails

This last doll is my favourite. You will notice that she is not a direct copy of the old kid-bodied dolls of the 19th and early 20th centuries, but has a look of the 1970's. This is because I have based my design on real-life proportions rather than on those used by Victorian dollmakers.

The style of hip joint used for this doll is known as 'ne plus ultra'. Although the stitched-on method was sometimes employed, hip joints were more usually fastened with rivet pins. The gusset knee and elbow joints used for this doll were also common, but the elbow gussets could be at the back rather than at the front.

The Victorian doll will appeal to children of all ages. It is easier to make than it looks but, if you are a beginner, I would suggest that you make one of the other dolls first.

Cutting out the pattern

Following the preparation instructions given on p. 12, cut out the pattern pieces.

Sewing

With the right sides of the calico together, sew along your pencil lines with a small running stitch [see p. 11].

The period appearance of the Victorian Doll is enhanced by the clothes, with lace trimmed petticoat and bloomers.

The legs

1 Sew separately the front seams, either side of the knees.
2 Cut the material along the knee joints between your pencil lines and backstitch [see p. 8] the gussets into position, so that the centre marks on the gussets match the seams [see figure 56].
3 Turn to the right side, ease the knees out to their correct shape and whip the seams [see p. 11].
4 With the right sides together again, sew down the backs of the legs.
5 Check that you have both a left and a right sole and stitch them into position.
6 Pin the rounded ends of the hip gussets to match the tops of the legs and sew them together, leaving about 5cm [2in] open at the back to allow for the stuffing [see figure 57].
7 Carefully turn the legs right side out again and whip the remaining seams.

The arms

1 Stitch the top inside seams down to the elbow. Fasten off. From the other side of the gusset, sew down to the wrist lines.
2 Cut the material between your pencil lines at the elbows and stitch the gussets in as for the legs.
3 Turn to the right side and whip these seams.
4 With the right sides together again, from the wrist line, stitch round the hands using backstitch, then use running stitch to sew up the rest of the arms.
5 Cut the material between the index fingers and the thumb on each hand.
6 Turn right side out, ease the thumbs out with a crochet hook and whip the remaining seams.

The body

1 Join the tops of the hips to the bottom of the two front body sections [see figure 58].
2 Turn to the right side and whip these seams.
3 With the right sides together, sew the centre front seam, turn to the right side and whip the seam.
4 Stitch the side gussets to this front section, gently easing them round the curves of the hips [see figure 59].
5 Matching the 'A' markings on the side and back sections, sew them together [see figure 60].
6 Sew up the remainder of the back seam.
7 Turn right side out and whip all these seams.

The head

Join the four sections, turn to the right side and whip the seams.

Fig 56

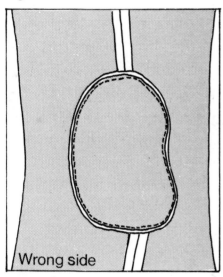

Wrong side

Fig 57

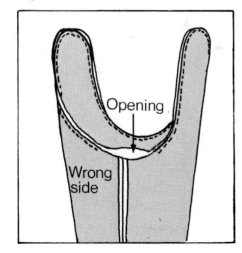

Opening

Wrong side

Stuffing

Before you begin this phase, read the general instructions on p. 14.

The legs

1 Stuff the feet and legs firmly up to the knee gussets.
2 Take one of the legs and, placing your thumb on the bottom half of the gusset to keep it flat, stuff really tightly across the top of it, well up to the front seam and then up the back of the knee.
3 Press more kapok up to the front seam of the upper gusset.
4 Hold the leg straight, with the gusset closed, and firmly stuff the remainder of the leg to the top of the centre front and back seams.
5 Turn in and oversew the opening.
6 Complete the other leg in the same way.

The arms

1 Place a small amount of kapok in the hands and work it well up to the finger seams.
2 Using a stabbing stitch [see p. 11], sew the three lines on each hand to make the individual fingers [see figure 61], following the markings on your paper pattern.
3 Place more kapok in the palms and, with the crochet hook, stuff it firmly into each thumb.
4 With a small running stitch, sew along the inside wrist lines as indicated on your paper pattern, from one seam to the other, slightly gathering the material. Fasten off the thread securely.
5 Continue stuffing up to the elbow gussets and work these as for the legs.
6 Finish stuffing the arms to within 13mm [½in] of the openings.

The body

1 Stuff both hips firmly.
2 Making sure that the legs are the right way round, stitch the inside leg tops to the inside of the hips [see figure 62], taking up all the thicknesses of material [use a darning needle and several lengths of thread]. Fasten the thread securely by knotting it a few times.
3 Continue to stuff the body as tightly as possible to just below the opening.
4 Holding the legs in a straight line with the body, pull the outside leg tops up the outside of the hips and stitch them as before [see figure 63].
5 Sew the tops of the arms to the side gussets along the openings [see figure 64].

Fig 58

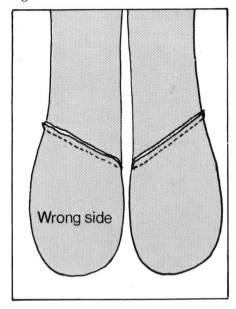

Wrong side

Fig 59

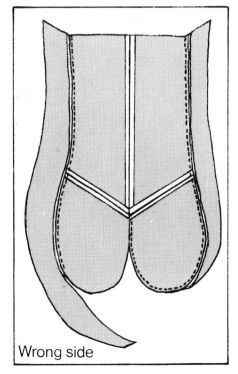

Wrong side

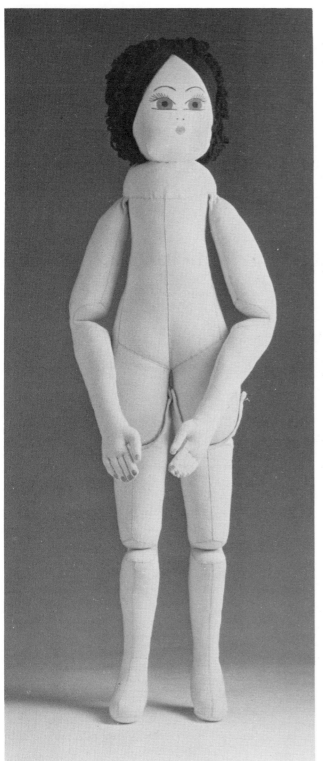
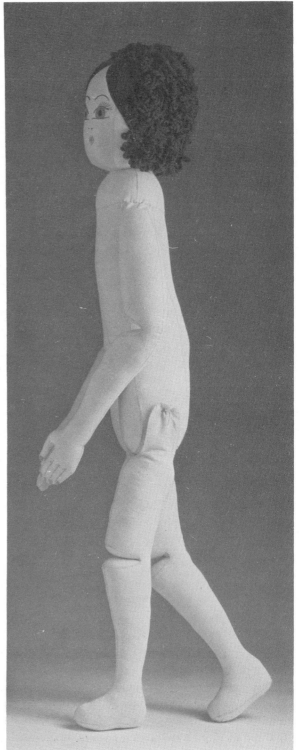

84

Three views of the more complex Victorian Doll. Note the gusseted elbow and knee joints, and the hip construction.

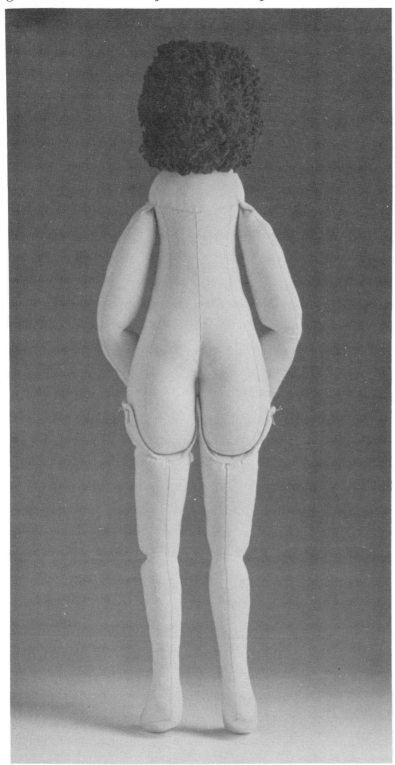

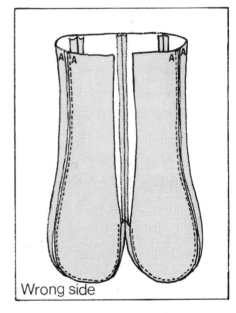

Fig 60

Wrong side

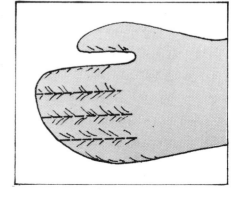

Fig 61

Fig 62

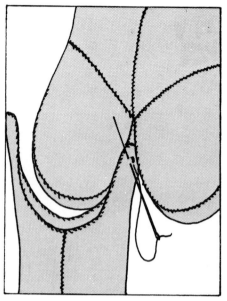

6 Stitch and whip the side seams of the shoulder section.

7 Turn in the bottom edge of this shoulder section 5mm [$\frac{3}{16}$ in] and tack it round with running stitch.

8 Pin this tacked edge onto the body [see figure 65] and oversew along the join.

9 Continue to stuff the body and shoulders right up to the neck opening.

The head

Stuff the head firmly, ensuring that one of the sections remains particularly lump free for the face.

Bringing your doll to life

1 Following the instructions given in Chapter Two, work the face.

2 Hold the head onto the neck at the most attractive angle. Tuck in the raw edges and stitch them together by sewing along the join several times until there are no gaps.

3 For the hair, follow the instructions given in Chapter Two.

4 Add the final touches by carefully painting the tips of each finger and thumb with pink nail varnish.

Dressing your doll

The Victorian doll looks best when dressed in long skirts and long-sleeved dresses that cover the knee and elbow gussets.

The patterns I have given can easily be adapted to make nightdresses and coats, or skirts and blouses.

Fig 63

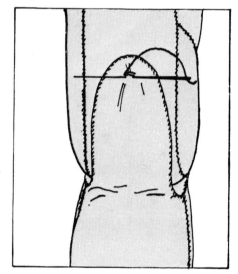

GIRL'S OUTFIT

As illustrated on p. 63.

Fig 64

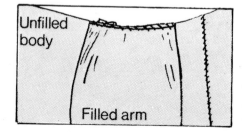

Materials required

Petticoat and pants
70cm of white cotton or lawn
Three small white buttons
120cm of narrow white lace

Dress with frill
70cm of fine terylene
Three small buttons

Pinafore
30cm of contrasting material
Two small matching buttons

Shoes or boots
Small pieces of leather or suede
Two small buttons [for the shoes]
1m of narrow ribbon
[for the boots]

Cutting out the pattern

Following the preparation instructions given on p. 22, cut out the pattern pieces.

Sewing

Sew 5mm [$\frac{3}{16}$in] in from the raw edges.

Petticoat

The bodice

1 Backstitch the shoulder seams to make two separate bodices [one bodice to form the lining]. Press open the seams.
2 With the right sides together, using a small running stitch, join the bodices along the neck and back edges.
3 Turn to the right side and press.
4 Turn in the armhole edges of both bodice and lining and oversew them together.
5 Join the side seams on the wrong side of the material. Turn back to the right side and press.

The skirt

1 Cut a length of material 33cm × 66cm [13in × 26in] and join the centre back with a french seam, leaving 12.5cm [5in] open at the top [see p. 21].
2 Turn in these raw edges and hem them down to make a neat opening.
3 With running stitch gather the top of the skirt to fit the bodice and then backstitch it to the bodice leaving the bodice lining loose [see p. 22]. Turn in the raw edge of the lining and hem it down to enclose the raw edges of the seam.
4 Work two buttonloops [see p. 22] on one edge of the back bodice and sew on the buttons.
5 Turn up and hem the skirt.
6 On the right side, just above the hemline stitching, make a small tuck in the material and sew along it with running stitch [see figure 66]. Press the tuck down towards the hem.
7 Stitch the lace, edge to edge, to the bottom of the hem.

Pants

1 With french seams, join the centre back and 5cm [2in] at the bottom of the centre front.
2 Turn in and hem these raw edges to make a neat opening.
3 Join the inside legs with a french seam and press.

The waistband

1 Cut a strip of material 2cm × 26cm [¾in × 10¼in].
2 With a small running stitch, gather the top of the pants to fit

Fig 65

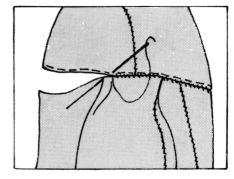

Fig 66

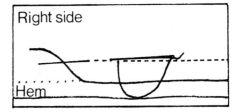

your doll and then backstitch the waistband to them, right sides together.

3 Fold the material over the raw edges of this seam, turn in the other edge of the waistband and hem it down to your original gather line. Tuck in and oversew the two ends.

4 Work a buttonloop on one end of the waistband and sew a button onto the other end.

5 Turn up and hem the legs. Press.

6 Stitch the lace to the bottom of the hems, edge to edge.

Dress with frill

The bodice

1 Backstitch all shoulder and side seams to make two separate bodices [one bodice to form the lining]. Press open all the seams.

2 With the right sides together, using a small running stitch, join the bodices along the neck and centre back edges.

3 Turn right side out and press.

The sleeves

1 Join with french seams and press them to one side.

2 Using a small running stitch, gather the tops of the sleeves to fit the armholes of the bodice. Backstitch them to the bodice, leaving the bodice lining loose [see p. 21].

3 Turn in the armhole edges of the lining and hem them down to enclose these seams.

4 Turn up and hem the cuffs. Press.

The skirt

1 Cut a length of material 28.5cm × 56cm [11¼in × 22in] and another length for the frill 6.5cm × 116cm [2¼in ×46in]. If your material is too narrow, cut two lengths and join them at the selvedges.

2 Gather one edge of the frill to fit the skirt, with running stitch, then, right sides together, join them with backstitch along the line of gathers.

3 On the wrong side, fold the material of the skirt down to cover this seam and hem it to the original line of stitching [see figure 67].

4 Use a french seam to join the centre back of the skirt and frill to within 12.5cm [5in] of the top.

5 Turn in the raw edges of this seam and hem them down to make a neat opening.

6 Gather the top of the skirt with small running stitches to fit the bodice, then backstitch it to the bodice, leaving the bodice lining loose.

Fig 67

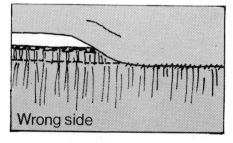

Wrong side

7 Turn in the raw edge of the lining and hem it down to enclose this seam.
8 Work three evenly-spaced buttonloops on one edge of the back bodice and sew the buttons into place.
9 Turn up and hem the frill. Press.

Pinafore

The bodice

1 Backstitch all the shoulder seams to make two separate bodices [one bodice to form the lining]. Press open all the seams.
2 With the right sides together, using a running stitch, join them along the neck and centre back edges.
3 Turn right side out and press.
4 Turn in the armhole edges of the bodice and the lining and neatly oversew them together on the right side.
5 On the wrong side, backstitch the two side seams. Fold them down and press on the right side.

The skirt

1 Turn up and hem the skirt from one side of the top round to the other.
2 Gather the top with running stitch so that it fits the bodice and backstitch it to the bodice, leaving the lining hanging loose.
3 Turn in the raw edge of the bodice lining and hem it down to enclose the raw edges of this join.
4 Work two buttonloops on one edge of the back bodice and sew the buttons into position. Press.

Shoes

1 Oversew the front and back seams.
2 Making sure that you have a left and a right sole, stitch them into place.
3 Make a buttonloop on the inside strap of each shoe and sew a button onto the other strap.

Boots

1 Oversew the front and back seams.
2 Stitch the left and right soles into position.
3 With a large darning needle pierce the holes for the laces as indicated on your paper pattern.
4 Sew in the tongues.
5 Ease the boots onto your doll, thread in the ribbons with a darning needle, and tie.

Petticoat skirt:
Cut one length of material
33cm x 66cm [13in x 26in]

Dress skirt:
cut one length of material
28.5cm x 56cm [11½in x 22in]
and another 6.5cm x 116cm
[2¼in x 46in]

Pinafore skirt:
cut one length of material
50cm x 25.5cm [20in x 10in]
fold in half and
shape the two bottom
corners

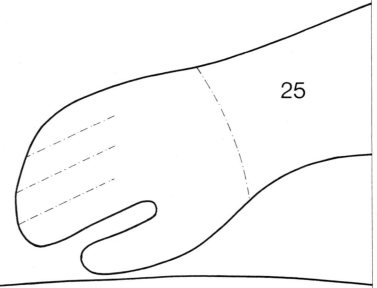

BEFORE CUTTING OUT:

Read chapter 1 (doll patterns)
Read chapter 3 (garment patterns)

25

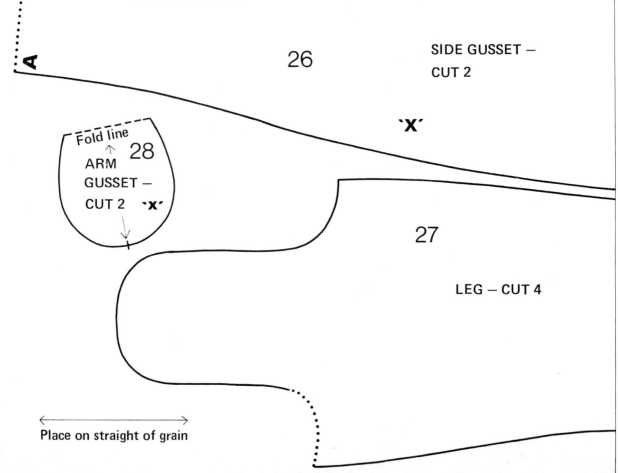

A

26

SIDE GUSSET –
CUT 2

`X´

Fold line
28
ARM
GUSSET –
CUT 2 `X´

27

LEG – CUT 4

← Place on straight of grain →

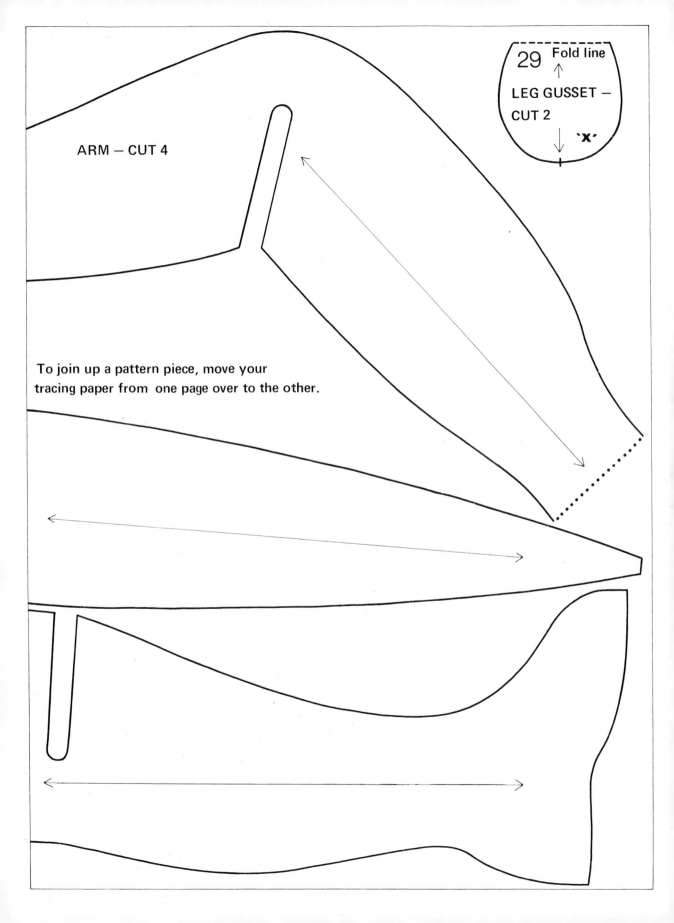

29 Fold line

LEG GUSSET —
CUT 2

`X`

ARM — CUT 4

To join up a pattern piece, move your
tracing paper from one page over to the other.

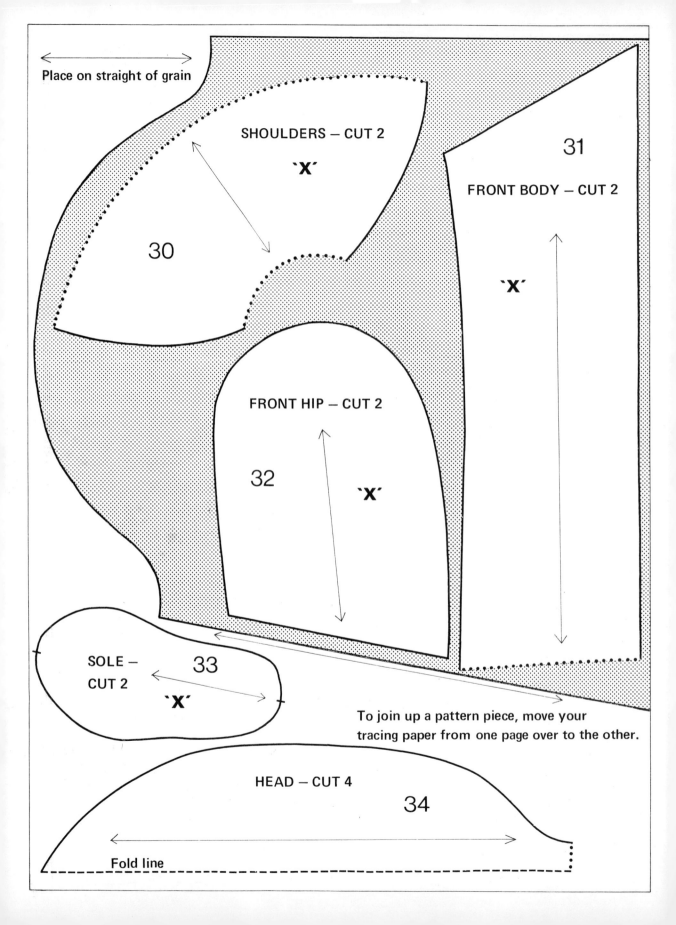

Place on straight of grain

SHOULDERS – CUT 2

`X`

30

31

FRONT BODY – CUT 2

`X`

FRONT HIP – CUT 2

32

`X`

SOLE –
CUT 2

33

`X`

To join up a pattern piece, move your
tracing paper from one page over to the other.

HEAD – CUT 4

34

Fold line

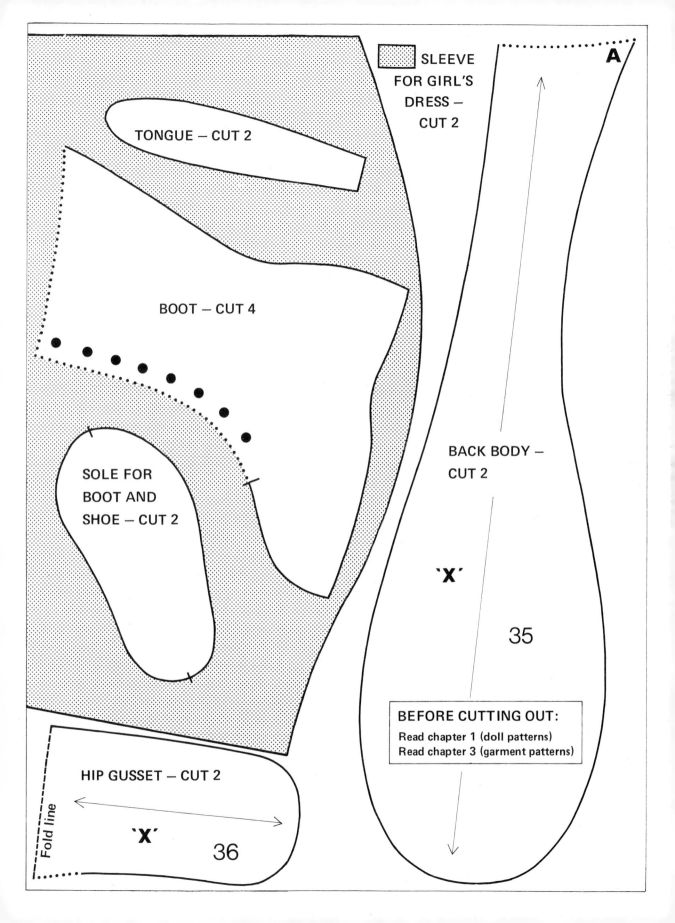

SLEEVE FOR GIRL'S DRESS — CUT 2

TONGUE — CUT 2

BOOT — CUT 4

SOLE FOR BOOT AND SHOE — CUT 2

BACK BODY — CUT 2

'X'

35

BEFORE CUTTING OUT:
Read chapter 1 (doll patterns)
Read chapter 3 (garment patterns)

A

HIP GUSSET — CUT 2

Fold line

'X'

36

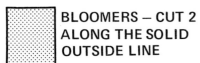 BLOOMERS — CUT 2
ALONG THE SOLID
OUTSIDE LINE

Place on straight of grain

To join up a pattern piece,
move your tracing paper from
one page over to the other.

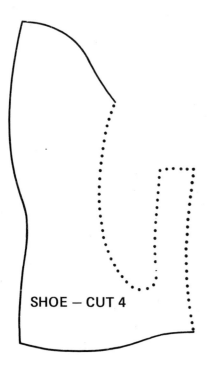

SHOE — CUT 4

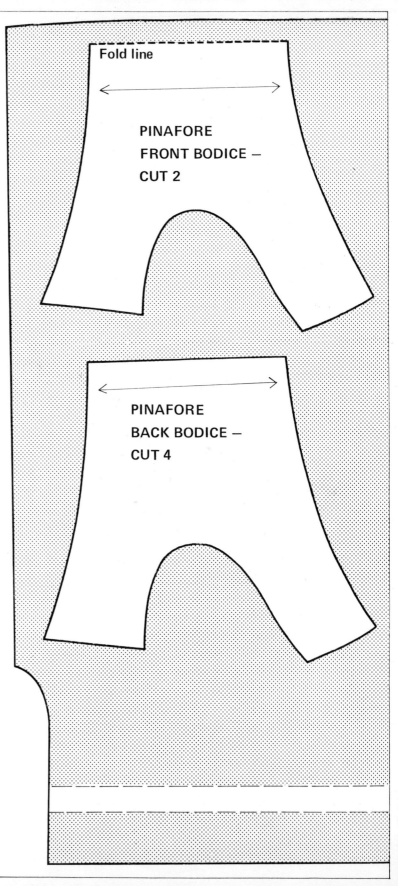

Fold line

PINAFORE
FRONT BODICE —
CUT 2

PINAFORE
BACK BODICE —
CUT 4

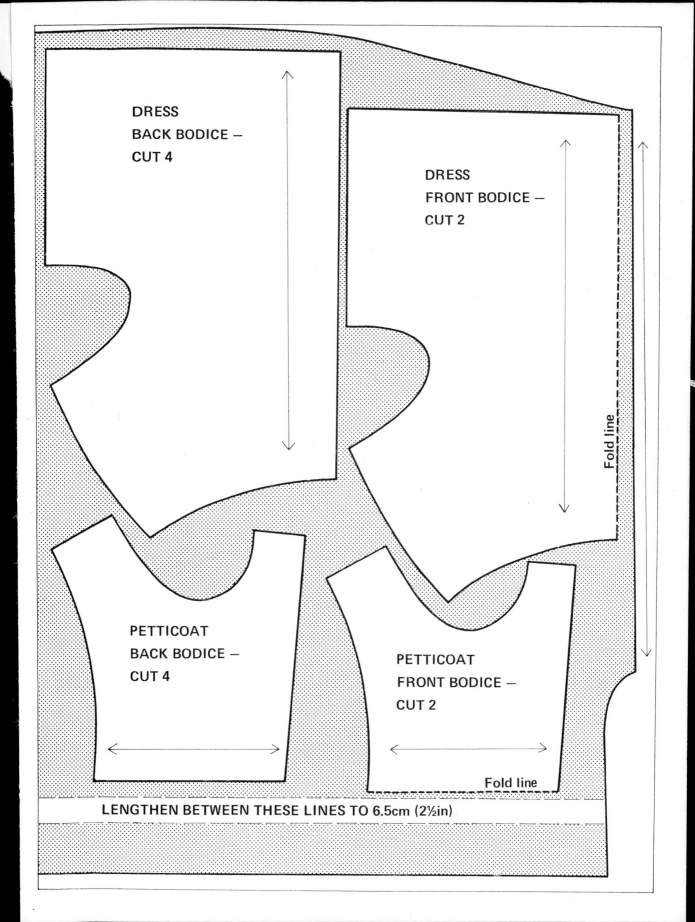

9. CARING FOR YOUR DOLL

With reasonable care your doll will last almost indefinitely and so, sooner or later, it will have to be cleaned.

If it is not too grubby you can wash it with warm soapy water, using a nailbrush to remove the dirt. Be careful not to get the doll too wet. Rinse off the soapsuds with a sponge and leave the doll to dry in a warm atmosphere.

It is obviously far better to clean your doll before it becomes really dirty. If, however, it suffers some accident, such as being dropped in a muddy puddle, it will require a thorough wash. In this case, scrub with a nailbrush dipped in warm, soapy water and then immerse it in clean water to rinse off the dirt. Dunk it up and down as quickly as you can—if you have followed the stuffing instructions carefully the water will take some time to penetrate the whole doll.

Remove the doll from the water, wrap it in a thin, clean cloth and place it in direct, very hot sunshine, on a radiator or in front of a fire. The doll must be dried *quickly* and in *direct* heat, otherwise the kapok will not return to its original state.